EXODUS, WANDERING AND TRIUMPH

James E. Kifer

New Harbor Press
RAPID CITY, SD

Copyright © 2025 by James E. Kifer.

All rights reserved. No part of this publication may be reproduced, distributed or transmitted in any form or by any means, including photocopying, recording, or other electronic or mechanical methods, without the prior written permission of the publisher, except in the case of brief quotations embodied in critical reviews and certain other noncommercial uses permitted by copyright law. For permission requests, write to the publisher, addressed "Attention: Permissions Coordinator," at the address below.

Kifer/New Harbor Press
1601 Mt. Rushmore Rd., Ste 3288
Rapid City, SD 57701
www.NewHarborPress.com

Ordering Information:
Quantity sales. Special discounts are available on quantity purchases by corporations, associations, and others. For details, contact the "Special Sales Department" at the address above.

Exodus, Wandering and Triumph / James E. Kifer. -- 1st ed.
ISBN 978-1-63357-466-3

Contents

PREFACE 1
LAND OF THE PHARAOHS 9
THE UNEQUAL CONTEST 23
LEAVING HOME 39
THE SCHOOLMASTER 63
A PATIENT GOD, AN EXASPERATED LEADER AND A
DISCONTENTED PEOPLE 73
COLLAPSE OF THE ISRAELITES 89
THE BANNERS OF REBELLION 103
FROM MOSES TO JOSHUA 117
JOSHUA LEADS THE WAY 131
THE SUN STANDS STILL 147
PARADISE LOST 165
THE LAND THAT WAS PROMISED 173
LEADERSHIP 187
QUO VADIS 201
CONQUER AND DIVIDE 213
COLLAPSE 229
MORE THAN CONQUERORS 245

PREFACE

Any author should commence a project with a twin spirit, each seemingly in conflict with the other. The scribe should have the confidence and belief in his own competence that his thoughts, his writing and his opinions can be sufficiently expressed to interest as many readers as possible. Seemingly, such a spirit of confidence is at variance with the other necessary spirit, that of humility, a firm belief that many others have trod the road before him and that their steps provide a lamp unto the author's feet. The present author is bold enough to both hope and suggest that he possesses a sufficiency of each spirit to make this volume worthy of reading and consideration.

Exodus, Wandering and Triumph is not a scholarly history of a subject to which many brilliant men and women have devoted their lives and careers to deep, thoughtful and exquisitely complex thought. For thousands of years this monumental story of the enslavement of the Hebrew people, their Divine emancipation, failures, long wanderings and eventual triumph in the Promised Land of Canaan has been the subject of massive scholastic work, be it religious or secular, and it has been the progenitor of volumes of work in many languages, but for our purposes most notably Hebrew, Greek and English. It remains (or at least should remain) a part of the curriculum in universities, and seminaries, and libraries should continue to burgeon with new volumes. Theologically, along with the Torah it remains the foundation of Orthodox Judaism and the moral and theological birthplace of what, for lack of better terms might be called "conservative" or "traditional" Christianity. The stories from two or three Biblical books show no signs of diminution in their attempted enlightenment of modern popular culture. Everything from classic Hollywood to whatever has followed in its glittering tinsel strewn path has attempted to make money from what was a relatively brief period, and geographically contained stage from thousands of years ago.

Neither is this a purely religious or theological work. Admittedly, this is a somewhat puzzling statement in that overwhelmingly the primary text for the history is found in two Old Testament books, Exodus and Joshua. Still the "secular" historical sources, be they Jewish, Egyptian, Canaanite or otherwise must be considered since our understanding is deepened by a grasp of their contributions. The detail and erudition of many historians, linguists, Biblical scholars and others on this period is so impressive that they should and must be considered.

Although many nations and their cultures will be considered the spine of the story is the tale of the Hebrew people and their sorrows, errors, blunders and triumphs against earthly odds that always appear to be some version or variation of the word "overwhelming," the cultures of others, especially the Egyptians and Canaanites are a requisite to the study. Also, it is among other things a story of the Ten Commandments, the Law of Moses and the almost incomprehensible reach of their influence upon humanity ever since.

This Preface has already asserted that the book is not a religious work. Still, it is short-sighted and well near impossible to speak and write at any length since the primary source is the most famous and widespread religious book in history, the Holy Bible. All the events of this history transpire at least one millennium before the Advent of Jesus Christ. To write of them, though, without at times seeing the foreshadowing of Christ and Christianity, events which such luminaries as Moses and Joshua never foresaw, is well-nigh impossible. The later coming of Christ as the true Light will be seen not as a shadow that falls over those Old Testament events but rather as the illumination that gives them real meaning. God's Light shown through the stories of His Chosen, the Hebrews, but the pure Light came not until later.

So, then, what is this volume intended to be? Its narrative structure will never be set adrift from the history of the nation of Israel, which provides the imperative for moving the story forward. The commencement is with the twelve sons of Israel (a/k/a more commonly Jacob), their necessary travels to the great land of Egypt, at that time by far the greatest power on this side of the earth, their travels, travails and eventual enslavement for four centuries by these same Egyptians who once welcomed them. Finally the God of Israel speaks, and the scene is set for perhaps the most dramatic series of clashes in history between an Egypt ruled by an absolute power in Pharaoh and the Israelites led by the most important man of the Old Testament, Moses. The stories which are born of this clash remain living tales whose permeation and roots are so deep that even today in a radically altered world their effects remain.

This long epic journey from the slavery in the sands of Egypt to the proverbial "milk and honey" of the Promised Land is impelled forward by both narrative and character. The story of the

Israelites alone is astounding in both the popular and scholarly interest it begets and the diabolically intense hatred it generates yet today. The believer accepts the Biblical narrative in full, while many skeptics still pay it homage by their fascination with the endless stories which never fail to excite interest. It begins with the violent hatred which ten young men held for their brother, their despicable treatment of him, the hellish darkness and gloom of slavery into which that one brother Joseph was seemingly condemned for life, and the Divine resurrection of the hopes and talents of this remarkable young man. The story of Joseph's family, which is that of the sons of Jacob, becomes one of familial love and understanding but simultaneously the shackles of national slavery will be forged for a period of four long, seemingly endless centuries of suffering. The story of the Israelites then becomes one in which the Divine Will of God emerges as more readily recognizable, and God's will and guidance becomes more directly, even miraculously displayed. Immortal God raises up a man who becomes probably the greatest leader of humanity the world has ever known, a man who by the time of his rebirth on the Biblical stage is merely a shepherd. We, of course, know him as Moses, perhaps the single most prominent figure in the old scriptures of the Jews. It is given to him burdens and responsibilities of leadership and shepherding never equaled before or since among men. He speaks for God, confronts rebellion which threatens to be ignited into a cauldron of revolution, knows disappointment, drudgery and endless disappointment during a long, long tenure of leadership. He defeats the most powerful man in the world, the Pharaoh of Egypt and then must contend with endless murmuring and rebellion among his own people. Remarkably and over decades he succeeds, but still God denies Moses the Promised Land, as He is now ready for another man to lead His Chosen nation, a man who brings honor to his name, and a name itself which will later be the most honored of all time. He is Joshua.

Joshua perhaps is one of the most underappreciated leaders and men in all Israel's history. He will be seen as astute and exceptionally well prepared for the leadership of Israel in one of the most critical times in its history, the conquest of Canaan. Joshua is proven as a magnificent leader, a general of the first rank and a man whose faith and devotion to God is unshaken and resolute. Under Joshua much of Israel will demonstrate a faith and strength theretofore lacking and not commonly seen thereafter.

Along the paths hopefully covered by this volume lie a multiplicity of miracles, battles, human confrontations, Divine love (and anger) and enough "action" seemingly to satisfy anyone. Except for its moment of origin, its "birth" into the world it is easier to overlook and even exclude something of monumental, lasting, history changing importance. It is the Law given to Moses on Mount Sinai, a law, legal and moral system which set the Israelites apart from all other people and the effects of which still permeate not just religion, but society in the twenty-first century. The Mosaical Law was the underpinning of the Jewish civilization and culture, but thankfully its historic, religious and cultural influence has never been limited to just one tiny nation on the shores of the eastern Mediterranean.

This period in Israel's history features so many famous persons, and in point, of fact, their number is not exclusive to Israel alone. Men such as Moses, Joshua and the Egyptian Pharaoh (likely Ramses II) are as fascinating and instructive today as they were during their lives. Others good, bad and otherwise have lasting fame or infamy and are marked by names such as Caleb, Aaron, Mirian, Rahab and Korah. Brief biographies of these persons hopefully will both reinforce traditional interpretations and also, without too much contradiction, add to our understanding of them by thorough analysis.

This is also intended to be a study of cultures, civilizations and the nature of the populations which peopled them and propelled them forth into history. Obviously, the Israelites, or Jews, or Hebrews, depending upon the preferred nomenclature of the moment will and should have center stage. Certainly, though, the story of Israel nor of ancient history, or at least this slice of it, cannot be understood without a comfortable familiarity of other people and civilizations, primarily the Egyptians and the Canaanites, but also such as the Amalekites and the Philistines. All were enemies to the Israelites, but that does not obliterate their cultural achievements, especially those of the Egyptians.

Undoubtedly, all the people, the populations of all countries, were daily living their lives and rarely, if ever, giving any consideration to such weighty and at times pretentious subjects as history, culture and religion. Remaining, though, always is the core and centrality of the fact that the small nation of Israel is not centrifugal but central to the story. Its appearance on the world stage is, to express in understatement, not world shaking at all.

The historical, though not the spiritual, tale of Israel's appearance upon the world stage and its importance and influence begins with an internecine story of brotherly jealousy which develops into hatred, a bitter gall that leads directly to slavery and the likely desired death of one of the brothers. The narrative thread broadens when that abused, enslaved brother is carted to mighty Egypt as so much chattel, presumably to perish within a few short years. Mighty Egypt becomes the vast stage upon which cataclysmic events will be writ large and played out for our consideration and God's will. It is in Egypt that the special nation of Israel really begins its struggle to be born, a goal and desire (of God's of course and occasionally even the Israelites) which is not realized until the appearance of a population and a nation yet unborn. The generation(s) which follow will be battle tested, battle worn and toughened, but finally a real nation, small, relatively powerless and somewhat insignificant to the powers of the day. It is a land of deep fissures, flaws and national character defects, but nonetheless as God's Chosen it prevails against a multiplicity of mortal foes.

Israel is intended by its Creator to be something special. It is a monotheistic land where only the one true God is to be recognized and worshipped. With that alone it is an island in a turbulent sea of polytheism, not just multiple gods and goddesses, but ferociously hostile polytheists. This tiny country is special in another way in that it possesses a legal and moral code of both amazing depth and Divine erudition. This code, known variously as the Law of Moses, the Torah, or in popular historical shorthand, The Ten Commandments makes Israel even more distinguishable from its neighbors.

Even the modern aggressively secularized world thinks of religion whenever (if ever) it turns its gaze and thoughts upon the worship of God, the distinctions that He provided for His people and the intellectual and spiritual treasures it received from God's Plan made ancient Israel into a structure and society which was a progenitor of something rarely attributed to it. With great but tempered acknowledgment and plaudits to the glory that was Greece and the grandeur that was Rome it is in early ancient Israel that the dim, adumbrated outlines of Western Civilization are first seen. It was marked by a comprehensive and equitable written code that gave glory and reverence to God and maximum freedom to the individual man and woman. The Law of Moses provided for a state sufficiently strong for all necessary purposes yet recognizing the individual freedom of each person. Perhaps modern political scientists would call it a "theocracy," but it was a theocracy that worked, giving glory to God and rights and dignity to humanity. It all began in a vast desert land of sand and stone.

CHAPTER ONE

LAND OF THE PHARAOHS

Some fourteen hundred years before the Advent of Christ the descendants of Jacob, now to be known as the Israelites, found themselves not only in a foreign land but an alien continent as well. From an obscure corner of southwestern Asia, known and still recognized by so many different names throughout history, Canaan, Israel, Palestine, the Promised Land, Judah, Judea, seemingly ad infinitum, the sons of the great Hebrew patriarch Jacob had come across borders and barriers, physical, cultural and spiritual and found themselves and their worldly salvation in the great northeastern African land of Egypt. Their story was, as are so many human tales, an epic of family and national tragedy and triumph, but one that played out under the auspices of God Himself and while not to be told as a full narrative deserves a brief summation.

Jacob, the aging patriarch, had two wives, two concubines, twelve sons and one daughter. The next to youngest son, Joseph, was a boy and then a man of superlatives. He was brilliant, hardworking, deeply spiritual and central to our story almost grotesquely the favorite of his father Jacob, and an object of intense jealousy and hatred by his ten older brothers. Narrowly escaping fratricide he was sold into slavery, taken to Egypt and through a torturous, fortuitous and Divinely directed life was taken on a path to the prime ministership of Egypt at age thirty. Back home a famine had befallen the land of Jacob and his family, and their hopes for survival lay in the granaries of Egypt, where sustenance had been stockpiled, at the Divinely directed behest of Joseph, for some seven years.

A series of events, complex, filled with emotion and pathos ensures, and Joseph and his brothers reunite in scenes of so much dramatic intensity that Shakespeare himself likely was amazed. To survive, Jacob, his sons, daughter Diana, and his now quite large extended family, immigrate from Canaan to Egypt, where they make a new home under the protective generosity of love of Joseph with the full blessings of Joseph's only superior on this earth, the Egyptian monarch known as the Pharaoh.

For a long period matters went well for the Israelites in their new Egyptian home, and they multiplied in numbers from a large patriarchal clan to a swelling, burgeoning nation. The first chapter of the Old Testament book of Exodus, itself perhaps the greatest adventure volume of all time, bespeaks that ominously portentous statement:

"Now there arose up a new king over Egypt, which knew not Joseph."

After generations the Israelites had ceased to be welcome guests and became, at least in the minds of the Pharaoh, a threat to his power. Powerful kings may be but surely nervousness, anxiety and fear are the great nullifiers of its enjoyment, as Pharaoh proclaimed to his fellow Egyptians:

"Behold the people of the children of Israel are more and mightier than we."

Whatever the relative populations of the Egyptians and the Israelites, Pharaoh still retained the power, the whip hand, and he showed no hesitancy in its application. Pharaoh had the army, the infrastructure of a powerful nation, and he subdued the Israelites by abject slavery. Later, the greatest of all Israelite leaders wrote with eloquence that Pharaoh "... set over them taskmasters to afflict them with their burdens" and they built the treasure cities of Pithon and Rameses. No matter what, though, no matter the bondage or the hard rigorous burdens of the Israelites they grew in population. Thus, Pharaoh's fears grew as well.

Often those with the greatest power and the most resources at their disposal are the most fearful. In plainer terms the high and the mighty frequently are cowards. Pharaoh found his solution to the population problem with the Israelites, and he decreed that all male Israelite babies were to be drowned. Countless Hebrew boy babies were cold bloodedly murdered by a man who had at his fingertips the command of mighty armies. Sometimes, though, matters go awry and the smallest, the least most humble person or thing can wreak havoc with the master plans of the mighty. A Hebrew couple from the tribe of Levi had a little boy baby and to spare his life he was placed in an ark of bulrushes which was then niched into the bank of the Nile River. Discovered there by none other than Pharaoh's daughter the baby, with his own Hebrew mother Jochebed nursing him, was taken into the Pharaoh's palace and raised as Egyptian royalty. The child was raised by the Pharaoh's daughter, and doubtless enjoyed all the delights and privileges of royalty and riches and was looked upon favorably by both the Egyptians and by God. In an irony that only the God of the Universe can engender while Pharaoh's servants and soldiers daily were slaughtering all Hebrew boy babies, in Pharaoh's house the mighty monarch was protecting, providing, likely even coddling, training and educating the one boy that to Pharaoh's purposes was necessary that he kill. The boy's name was Moses. The baby, child, youth and young man Moses grew up in a protected environment with all the advantages that the most advanced civilization in the world, Egypt, could then provide, and surely, he lacked for little or nothing. He, an Israelite, was a member of the royal family, and life provided succor, luxury, riches and advantages that were available to but a few.

An old adage dating back several millennia is that "Egypt is the Nile, and the Nile is Egypt." At times, adages, folk wisdom and the like can be more true than false, and this saying had (and to some measure retains) a central truth. Without the great Nile River, the longest in the world, traversing Egypt in a south to north direction, the mystic and mythical civilization of Egypt would be one almost endless sand dune. Outside the Nile and its basin to a large measure this is true. The great river, the world's longest, begins in the heart of sub-Saharan Africa, widens, narrows, curves, bends through over four thousand miles of territory until it empties into the Mediterranean Sea on the northern coast of Egypt. When it flows through Egypt it flows through the expanse of the seemingly endless sands of the Sahara Desert. Yet it transforms what it touches for a considerable distance on either side, and the Nile River Valley was and remains abundantly fertile. As it approaches the Mediterranean it divides into a number of tributary streams forming the Nile Delta, upon which was built one of antiquity's greatest cities, Alexandria.

Within the borders of the Nile Valley and Nile Delta the land of Egypt became rich and, in some places, and aspects even luxurious. Most importantly it became the great granary, or breadbasket, of this portion of the ancient world. It produced food for itself and in the good years a generous surplus desired by others, not least among them the sons of Jacob. A millennium after the events of our story it became a ripe plum to be picked by mighty Rome for many reasons, not least of which was the agricultural harvest which beckoned.

History shows that many countries have been well favored by God and God's nature and have done little with the resources with which they were blessed. The ancient Egyptians escape this historical critique, though, and their glory in antiquity, lasting in some measure for over three thousand years is mightily impressive. The Egyptians were an artistic people, and their drawings, paintings, buildings, and architectural innovations and designs are impressive even in this age of advanced technology. Technologically, they were almost preternatural in some of the advancements they forwarded. From the reeds of the papyrus plant, ubiquitous on the banks of the Nile, they developed an early form of writing paper which allowed the ancients to record their thoughts and deeds on a surface other than stone or wood. Perhaps even more fascinating, and so it remains to us in the twenty-first century is that the Egyptians developed the art of embalming to preserve the bodies of the dead, even is a wickedly hot climate.

Were these ancient Egyptians some sort of super men and women, different than other humans? Not hardly. They were not a pure race or nationality (as if there was such a thing) but primarily a mixture of Hamites and Semites, two of the sons of Noah, and the latter being the progenitor of the Israelites as well. Those who study such matters have estimated that the typical Egyptian man was about 5"6" tall and the women perhaps 5"0", small in modern societies, but not particularly so in antiquity. Generally they were a slender people with fine facial features, certainly not as fair as the average European, but not particularly dark complexioned either. The ancient Egyptians were not the modern Egyptians. In the first few centuries A.D. various Middle Eastern people, primarily of Arabic origin, migrated to Egypt, and the ancient Egyptians were absorbed and displaced.

To this moment, though, without doubt the object and/or accomplishment most associated with ancient Egypt is one of the Seven Wonders of the World, the Pyramids of Giza, the greatest of these breathtakingly awesome structures constructed by the Egyptian pharaohs, one to two millennia before the children of Jacob even came to the land searching for food. They are spread throughout nine "communities" of these structures, and their awe-inspiring wonder still leaps from the pages of their photographs. They were constructed as tombs for the Pharaohs, to commemorate their lives and even their deaths and places in society which could never be extinguished. The Great Pyramid itself consumed twenty years in its construction, and its pinnacle is almost 500 feet in height. Many pyramids took even longer to construct, and these giant structures of limestone and sandstone were fashioned only by the most primitive ancient tools. And... slave labor, almost in inconceivable quantities. Though the time of their construction was long before the coming of the Israelites, the pharaohs had an endless work schedule of other great buildings, structures and monuments awaiting their sweat and labor.

For its time and place the engineering and structural skills of the Egyptians were nothing short of magnificently grand. Their pyramids, monuments and much of their city structures remain thousands of years later. Still, for all their genius and innovation their accomplishments would be minuscule except for two factors. Egypt was a great, growing military power which was in the habit of defeating its enemies. Secondly, it had the national will and power to enslave their defeated opponents. Much of Egypt's grandeur was built upon the breaking and broken limbs of slaves, most particularly the Hebrew slaves. The concept of free labor of "foreigners" and "aliens" would have been anathema to the Egyptian masters. Well and succinctly did the Hebrew Book of Exodus express their misery:

> "And they made their lives bitter with hard bondage, in mortar, and in brick, and in all manner of service in the field; all their service, wherein they made them serve, was with rigor."

For four centuries it continued until a free Israel was a far distant historical memory, until now when the Israelites had been ground to resemble the grains of sand which surrounded them.

The vast slave population of Israel apparently faced little or nothing but misery, degradation and short, bleak futures. They were totally leaderless, helpless, and the Deity who they so honored had been silent for some four centuries. A popular rebellion would have been laughingly absurd. Help and salvation could not come from within, but must be provided from without.

The baby Moses had grown up in Egyptian culture and Egyptian tutelage, but in the fullness of his youthful prime tragedy occurred. Raised an Egyptian aristocrat he had not forgotten that he was Hebrew, and the day came when the dichotomy of nations would have an open realization. One day he saw an Egyptian overseer beating a fellow Hebrew. To save the Hebrew Moses killed the offending Egyptian, but to his chagrin it was not done in private. Two days later a fellow Hebrew confronted Moses, as Moses attempted to break up a fight between the man and a fellow Hebrew. Undoubtedly Moses was shocked when the man confronted him with:

> "Who made thee a prince and a judge over us? Intendest thou to kill me, as thou killest the Egyptian? And Moses feared and said, Surely this thing is known."

The news reached Pharaoh, and Moses was now a wanted man, already condemned without trial by the Egyptian "god." He became a fugitive and fled across the desert to the land of Midian. There Moses married a woman named Zipporah, became a shepherd, and doubtless lived this middle portion of his life with respect and prosperity. It was a far cry from Egyptian courts and pageantry, but Moses settled into a hard working but pleasant life, a life which brought him contentment. Still, his fellow Hebrews suffered under Pharaoh and the lashes of his taskmasters. The Lord of Hosts, though silent for a time, had not removed Himself from the scene.

What is perceived as silence by God is never permanent, and the silence was about to end with a major step forward in God's Plan for Redemption. On just another workday when Moses had led a flock of his sheep to Mount Horeb "... an angel of the Lord appeared unto him in a flame of fire out of the midst of a bush." Thus began a conference between God and man, in this case Moses, unparalleled in all history. The story, known for so long and so well, by many, is condensable to an understanding that God revealed that He had selected Moses to return to Egypt, assume leadership of the Israelites, defeat Pharaoh and return to the mountain to worship Him. Moses, reverent to God though he was, by now he thought of himself as a simple shepherd, not particularly articulate, certainly no great speaker, and he was aghast and terrified that his Lord had selected him for such a monumental feat, which undoubtedly, he believed was impossible.

Egypt was not to be subdued by a great army led by anyone, including Moses. Israel was a slave nation totaling lacking in military acumen and resources. Its population was small compared to Egypt, and if Moses had ever possessed the skills of a general, such had long since atrophied. He was no eloquent orator, he himself pleading that he was "slow of speech." Besides, unlike what cinema and television programs have long showed Moses would be confronting a Pharaoh who was a stranger to him. He made these arguments, which we are reluctant to call excuses, because each one has a logic supporting it. Still, God's patience, is usually of long duration. Inally, after Moses had produced an almost encyclopedic list of reasons "... the anger of the Lord was kindled against Moses when this long-time shepherd finally suggested that God find another man for this undertaking:

> "And the anger of the Lord was kindled against Moses, and He said, Is not Aaron the Levite thy brother? I know that he can speak well. And also, behold, he cometh forth to meet thee: and when he seeth thee, he will be glad in his heart."

As a petulant, reluctant child who knows that he has pushed a parent as far as he can be pushed, Moses knew that his session with the Heavenly Father was over. Thus he retreated and returned to the tent and presumed safety of his father-in-law Jethro.

Moses, now a man of accomplishment and prosperity was about to take the first steps into the final third of his life, a journey in which he would free Israel, forward the nation of Israel and move not just Israel but all mankind dramatically forward to its ultimate redemption a thousand years hence. But who was Moses really, and what was he thinking?

Contemplating and then declaring the thoughts of any man or woman is a perilously hazardous undertaking. It has been the bane of many literary and dramatic works wherein their author attempts to reveal the thought processes of real, actual human beings. How is an author, three thousand years removed from the scene, possibly conversant with the thoughts and mental processes of an actual historical figure? The answer is that only with the greatest difficulty may they be discerned, but sometimes the facts and the person's present and future actions reveal his thoughts, at least in part.

Moses had awakened that morning, and as most persons he had at least a general; if not even a partially or perhaps wholly specific idea and plan for his day. He was an enterprising and successful shepherd, totally removed from the main arena and thoroughfares of political, military and after a fashion even religious affairs in the ancient world. He had a beloved wife, two sons, respect from his neighbors and associates, and was living a quiet, perhaps at times a bit of a monotonous life, but he was safely ensconced in domestic tranquility. The days of royal Egyptian palaces, pharaohs, princes, princesses, antiquity's, great and the good were so long past they were practically the memories of another man. He was now charged, commissioned and assigned to return to it, not as its royal beneficiary but as its antagonist.

Moses knew that he had skills, but they were the skills of a pastoral shepherd, a husband, a father and likely a man of standing and some influence among the people with whom he lived. As with all the truly great and the good, though, Moses possessed qualities of which he was either unaware or of which he had little notice. Although he quibbled with God, he was a man of faith in God. While he may have offered God excuses, he never offered refusal. While it is generally unspoken, Moses had no doubts that God was doing what was needed, but rather Moses's doubt (almost a certainty) was that he was not the right man for the endeavor. At long last talking, debating, kibbitzing (a later invented Jewish term), moping, excuses, ad nauseum had to end, and so they reached their terminus. So, this long scene ended:

> "And Moses took his wife and his sons, and set them upon an ass, and he returned to the land of Egypt: and Moses took the rod of God in his hand."

Actually, Moses's "work order," if such it could be called can be expressed with a general simplicity and understanding. He was to return to an amorphous group of people, the Israelites, slaves to the core of their being and such for our four centuries, free them, lead them across a desert to the mountain where God first appeared to Moses, and where God would begin to make of them a real nation.

Naturally, Moses had to obtain the license of the slaves' owner, the Egyptian pharaoh, an absolute ruler and the most powerful man in the world, a man who knew neither Moses nor the God of Moses. At his command Pharaoh had the support of an advanced ancient civilization and the world's most powerful army. Moses, a shepherd, had the companionship and assistance of his younger brother Aaron, a man just as powerless but well-spoken and articulate. True, Moses had the multitudes of Israelites at his back if he could persuade them to follow, but for now and actually for a very long time to come his own people were not an asset, but rather a responsibility, a burden and eventually even a liability. Scared, fearful, nervous, apprehensive, and all the linguistic cohorts of these words was Moses. With the singular exception of the Great Story of humanity's redemption by its Savior some fourteen hundred years later Moses had been given the greatest task and responsibility any man or woman has ever received.

When Moses was directed to return to Egypt he was led by God back to a civilized land, but civilized only in a pre-Christian sense. As has been noted Egypt had developed through countless centuries arts and sciences, both aesthetically and practically that surpassed all other extant cultures. Although Egypt certainly was a pagan land the Egyptian people and culture rightfully could claim to be religious. The wonders and accomplishments of the Egyptians may be praised, lauded and extolled, but certain salient facts cannot be avoided. Egypt was ruled by a "man-god," the king, potentate, emperor, or whatever title he might claim. He was the pharaoh, his power was absolute, unchallengeable and unchanging, and of all this Pharaoh (the name by which this work will call him) was well aware. Life, death, favor, disfavor, slavery, freedom, and on without end were at his fingertips and could be directed by his whim. His military forces were mighty, and as they were feared, so was he. Further, he had the backdrop, prestige and power of two thousand years of history, and all this and more put mighty winds in the royal sails.

Moses feared what the future held for him. The scriptures are so expressive that little doubt can be found that Moses did not feel himself up to a task greater than any man had ever been given. Pharaoh, though, was blissfully unaware of what lay ahead for both Egypt and himself. Nonetheless, Moses readied himself, his wife and family and began the long trek across the desert sands to the columned halls of Egypt. A cataclysmic crash was in the offing, and the contest to see who was God in Egypt was about to begin.

CHAPTER TWO

THE UNEQUAL CONTEST

The background and raison d'etre for the clash between not just two peoples, two cultures and two nations has been painted. All these factors are certainly in the mix but the real contest, the great point of contention, will be a conceptual question far above any of this. Was mankind created or did he appear, or did he evolve solely for the purpose of serving other men, to be ordered about, controlled, censored or pushed and shoveled about like heaps of undistinguishable dead flies to return to the void of nothingness after they had served their earthly masters and "betters?" Or were men and women created free in the image of their Creator, the one true God, to serve and glorify Him by worship and obedience which simultaneously glorified the worshipper? Did man exist to serve Pharaoh or to serve God? This was the question, still extant at all times and in all earthly places. One of its first and still most dramatic arenas of contest would be in Egypt and its two great earthly protagonists were Pharaoh and Moses.

So, what were the odds? For the contest laden modern world, be it sports, politics or any point in between the gambling odds makers are always studying and contemplating the odds for any pending contest. The salient question here is whether Moses would be able to free upwards of a million Hebrew slaves from the four-hundred-year strangling grasp of the Egyptian Pharaohs. Any detailed review of the assets and liabilities which Pharaoh and Moses brought into the clash would now be repetitive, tedious and superfluous. Let us be frank, terse and succinct. By all earthly calculations the odds were incalculable, and Moses had no possible route of Freedom for his fellow Israelites. Pharaoh held all the cards, all the assets, and Moses none. Actually at Pharaoh's command Moses could have been ground down to the consistency of the Egyptian desert sands.

Be that as it may and with the blessings of his Midianite father-in-law Moses, after decades' absence, returned to Egypt, accompanied by his wife Zipporah, his two sons and carrying a shepherd's staff. Of the two men, Pharaoh and Moses, Pharaoh, absolute ruler of the world's strongest nation and Moses, a one-time potential Hebraic/Egyptian rising star but now a humble shepherd lacking in self-confidence presented a ridiculous mismatch, one which was really no contest at all. None at all except that Pharaoh never realized, or if he did it was too late, that his opponent was not Moses but rather the God of Moses. Moses had his shepherd's rod, but the real shepherd's rod was Moses himself, and the true shepherd was God. The earthly odds which awarded in advance the contest to Pharaoh of a truth, actually were reversed. In a contest between Pharaoh and God the contest was actually nowhere to be found. God had already determined that the victor in this contest was to be God Himself. But the contest, the echoes of which reverberate still, had yet to unfold.

Actually, the steps of Moses would not be those of a solitary figure. God directed his older brother Aaron, a Levite priest, to meet Moses at Mt. Sinai, from whence Aaron would join Moses in the procession to Egypt. First, the two brothers went to the elders of the Israelites, conferred with them and informed them of God's plans. Moses performed miracles before them, they believed, as did the people of Israel themselves and:

> "(W)hen they heard that the Lord had visited the children of Israel, and that He had looked upon their affliction, then they bowed their heads and worshipped."

Likely, Moses' self-doubts were fading a bit and his self-confidence growing. He already had the commission of God Himself, and now the Israelites appeared to be offering him substantial popular support. At least, that is, for the moment. The moment for that first meeting of Pharaoh and Moses was now at hand. For the Hebrew slaves it would be a catastrophe literally of historic proportions.

Drama cannot sustain itself indefinitely, and the scene for the first great confrontation finally had arrived. Into the palace of Pharaoh came two apparently non-descript Hebrew shepherds, the brothers Moses and Aaron and in a moment of repeated artistic, literary and cinematic grandeur went before the mighty king and they:

> "(T)old Pharaoh, Thus saith the Lord God of Israel, Let my people go that they may hold a fast unto me in the wilderness."

Whatever Moses expected he certainly received no religious epiphany from Pharaoh, for the king haughtily answered:

> "Who is the Lord that I should obey His voice to let Israel go? I know not the Lord, neither will I let them go."

Not only haughty but also cruel to a degree that is born only of power. A great mass of the Israelites were construction workers, expendable slaves utilized to fashion the monuments and buildings of the great Egyptian land. Brusquely he ordered his henchmen:

> "And Pharaoh commanded the same day the taskmasters of the people, and their officers saying Ye shall no more give the people straw to make brick, as heretofore; let them go and gather straw for themselves."

The diversity and magnitude of the power which lay behind two men, Pharaoh and Moses, was so great that it is only with a strain of credulity that the coming events could be called a contest. Yes, the struggle over the question of slavery or freedom would go forward for quite some time, but its end was certain and clear. In this ridiculously, ludicrously unequal contest between Pharaoh and Moses, it was Moses who was already destined to win. Actually, the impending result was clear to everyone, but to only one correctly. Pharaoh heard not these words but the ominous portent to him was deeply foreboding:

> "Then the Lord said unto Moses,

> Now shalt thou see what I will do Pharaoh, for with a strong hand shall he let them (the Israelites) go, and with a strong hand shall he drive them out of his land."

To Pharaoh and to his Egyptian subjects the man and his office, together the very images of earthly and transcendent power, had merged into one, and Pharaoh himself was seen as divine. Not so, said the God of Abraham, Isaac and Jacon and now Moses. God promised to harden the heart of Pharaoh and:

> "... the Egyptians shall know that I am the Lord, when I stretch forth mine hand upon Egypt, and bring out the children of Israel from among them."

Before, however, Moses came to death grips with Pharaoh he learned of another enemy, an enemy so implacable yet resilient, so resentful, vengeful and actually childish that Moses would be forced to contend with them for the remaining forty years of his life. Sadly, but truly that enemy was his own people, his fellow Hebrews.

Following the disappointing debut meeting of Moses and Aaron with Pharaoh and his edict of punishing the Israelites by adding to their burdens the Israelite elders met with the two brothers and issued to Moses a wish for his condemnation:

> "The Lord look upon you, and judges because ye have made our savior to be abhorred in the eyes of Pharaoh, and to the eyes of his servants, to put a sword in their hand to slay us."

With this reaction from the Israelite leaders, whether he knew it or not, Moses had just received the news that for the remaining forty years of his life his greater problem would not be the Pharaoh or his Egyptian subjects but rather his own fellow Israelites. Therein will lie much of the story that follows, but for the moment Moses still had to turn his face to Pharaoh and the yet extant slavery of the Israelites. The real contest between Pharaoh and Moses was about to commence, and Pharaoh had already experienced his final day of victory. God's plan was to commission Moses and Aaron as His agents to lead the entire Israelite people from the shackles of slavery by an exodus from Egypt and ultimate triumph in the Promised Land, all of those events which would foreshadow far greater ones to come. God did not skimp in the power, status and prestige which He conferred upon Moses and his brother:

> "The lord said unto Moses,
> See, I have made thee a god to Pharaoh; and
> Aaron, thy brother, shall be thy prophet."

He promised Moses that Moses's speech was the conduit through which God would state His plans to Pharaoh, and then issued a momentous statement that was both an edict and a statement of intent:

> "And I will harden Pharaoh's heart, and multiply
> my signs and wonders in the land of Egypt.
> And the Egyptians shall know that I am the Lord,
> when I stretch forth mine hand against Egypt,
> and bring out the children of Egypt from among
> them."

God, the Creator of all men and women, the breather of life, omniscient and omnipotent, recognized traits in the pinnacle of His creation, man, that have never been absent. One factor, deplorable and despicable yet evergreen among all generations, is that those with power rarely and gracefully relinquish that power. Those with great power even more so. None had greater power than Pharaoh, and he was about to experience a display of real power that strongly reverberate yet today. A man with the putatively absolute power of Pharaoh held his authority and mastery of all so closely, tightly, and majestically that he had to be pummeled, trampled and even humiliated before an iota of this life sustaining sustenance of raw power would be released. He was now to receive all these and more, and they would come from the hands of two brothers from an Israelite tribe of slaves, the Levites, two brothers who had achieved earthly obscurity. Yes, Moses had once had some renown, but this was two generations past, and Aaron as a slave had no standing with the Egyptians. God saw that this also took a bit of time, but at its conclusion Egypt would be wrecked, Pharaoh diminished, and God exalted. In the end Pharaoh and the Egyptians would know that the God of Moses and Aaron was God.

The arsenal which God employed to level Egypt and Pharaoh was not one of spectacular, dazzling displays of glory or grandiosity, not healings, resurrections, choruses of angels singing or any such heavenly power. God's earthly right hand was Moses, and his weapon was human misery, not pretty, not attractive, but repulsive, hideous and grotesque. Egypt, including and especially Pharaoh, was about to be whipped, abused and brought low by a series of ten miseries, all spiritually and physically repugnant. They are not known, however, as the Ten Miseries but rather then and forever after as the Ten Plagues of Egypt. In rapid succession the populace of Egypt was afflicted with nine plagues, not imaginary, not ethereal, not emotional or psychological (though these definitely were part of the real fabric of suffering), but actual physical and physically repulsive epidemics. The list is filled with such human delights as water all turning to blood, the ubiquity of frogs, then of gnats, the death of valuable livestock, the Egyptian people being afflicted with boils on their skin, hail which turned to fire when it descended, and continual darkness in the land.

Pharaoh, like all tyrants, despots and their "wannabes" could not abide alternative, competing sources of power. Now, he by his intransigence when Moses and Aaron first confronted him, had brought down upon himself and his people the terrors of hell itself, and to which he had no answer but a strange consistency of behavior. Perhaps even in this most famous of stories, though, it is too easy to over emphasize the personality and character of Pharaoh and at times even Moses at the expense of the true antagonist, God Himself, the author of the plagues of Egypt.

What befell the earth, the land, Egypt and Pharaoh was cruel, physically horrendous and in many cases impossible to bear. Did this come from a loving and forgiving God or from the wrath of a vengeful Deity. Actually, to say either is to relegate the plagues to whimsical, haphazard events, when they were really major elements in God's plan of ultimate redemption. The ensuing period of distress for the land of Egypt, and it must be said for the Israelites as well, is to be understood as a clash, even a war, between two rival theologies, and thus bears brief examination.

Among the ancients the Egyptians should be considered a "religious" people, but not just religious in the sense that they constructed a few stone idols and obelisks, gave them names and then went about their own worldly ways, unchecked by any sense of moral obligation. In Egyptian theology their concept of the divine was not wholly removed from the daily lives of people. In some ways (and too much should not be made of this) the Egyptian religion bore a bit of similarity to the Hebrew's practice of monotheism. The Hebrews and their spiritual descendants worshipped the one true God from which all life emanates and all blessings flow. Only He is divine, and only He ("Yahweh" to the Hebrews) is to be acknowledged as God. The Egyptians did not focus nor recognize such exclusive power in one deity, but generally throughout their history they accorded supreme power to one god, generally known as Amon-re, the sun god. While Amon-re was supreme their religion left room for many gods of subordinate and specialized powers. This people, whose life and sustenance came from the Nile River, worshipped that greatest of all waters from which sprang their very existence. Without the Nile Egypt was but a fantasy.

To the Egyptians the great life-giving entities were the Nile and the sun, whose warming rays and energies combined with the flowing waters of the Nile gave birth and life to this grand civilization which was otherwise surrounded and imprisoned by the Sahara Desert. Through the seemingly endless years of the developing grandeur of Egypt their theological system made room for multiple deities, most based upon life and nature. The Egyptians cherished and bowed down before various deities of nature, gods and goddesses of nature of plants and all sorts of animals, including not just the higher breeds but such creatures as insects, spiders and yes, even snakes. Gods, goddesses, priests, religious shrines, pyramids, monuments, etc., everywhere. Egypt truly was a religious nation, proudly religious and possessor of the one man on earth who himself was a god, Pharaoh.

Pharaoh and Egypt retained a literal death grip upon the vast numbers of Hebrew slaves. If that grip was to be loosened and ultimately released Egypt's very heart had to be pierced, and that heart was its religion. The apex of that pyramidal religion was not just Amon-re but the Pharaoh himself. With all its power, panoply and glory, though, the God of Moses ordained that it was time for the edifice to begin to crumble. Thus, the plagues, and their effect, had they been known in advance, would have been horrible to contemplate. The plagues began and ended with blood.

All the water, the previous life giving and sustaining water of Egypt, was for seven days turned into blood. The scriptures themselves most eruditely, yet eloquently, tell how the plagues began:

> "Thus saith the Lord,
> In this shalt thou know that I am Lord: behold, I will smite with the rod that is in my hand upon the waters which are in the river, and they shall be turned to blood.
> And the fish that is in the river shall die, and the river shall stink; and the Egyptians shall loathe to drink of the water of the river."

So Moses and Aaron did as told, and the mighty Nile as well as all streams, pools, lakes and ponds that were once the sources of life-giving water were filled with the grotesque sight and foul odor of blood. The Egyptian god of the Nile, a deity named Happi, apparently was no match for Jehovah. Seven days of almost unimaginable, putrid horror beset Egypt and Pharaoh, but still the mighty king's heart remained hardened, and the Israelites remained slaves. Pharaoh's hardened heart signaled the onset of the second plague, one annoying, frightening, abhorrent and ultimately terrifying. Frogs. From the great Nile sprang not relief, but:

> "... frogs abundantly, which shall go up and come into thine house, and into the bedchamber, and upon thy bed, and upon the house of thy servants, and upon the people, and into thine ovens, and into thy kneading troughs."

The disgust of being surrounded, trampled upon and sickened by these revolting and now ubiquitous animals must have been repugnant and nauseating. It, too, though, held a place in the pantheon of Egyptian deities, known as the goddess Heqet, she of the divinity of frogs. The God of Moses had turned yet another Egyptian deity against, blood and now frogs being too much. Pharaoh saw that his great land had begun to suffer blows, its people suffering and in many cases dead. Pharaoh himself begged for relief from Moses, and within twenty hours the plague of frog ceased. The aftermath is tersely, yet somewhat colorfully, described in one sentence from Exodus:

> "(T)hey gathered the (frogs) together upon heaps; and the land stank."

Finally, Pharaoh implored relief from Moses and his God and promised to release the Israelites from bondage. A human being, though, be he prince or pauper, is an amazing creature of so many elements, often in conflict one with another. Quickly, the horrors of the blood and the frogs began to fade and subside from Pharaoh's memory and conscious thought until his mind was changed. No, he said, I will not release them, and they shall continue to serve as a slave nation to my throne and the people of Egypt.

God's arsenal, though, was still replete with His weaponry. In succession as the night follows the day came other plagues, the next being an infestation of pestilence and filth in the form of lice, for which the Egyptians worshipped yet another god, God, yes, the god of lice. It was a miserable time in Egypt, and Pharaoh again cried "I surrender." Again, though, he had a rapid change of his dark heart and clung to the Israelites like a child grasping a toy.

Tedious it would be to recite the story of the arrival and departure of the ensuing six plagues because it is literally the same story, different verse. The next six times, the tale of Pharaoh's intransigence hardened heart leading to the devastation and suffering of the Egyptian, but not the Israelite, population. It is also the story of the humbling and humiliation of the heathen deities in which Pharaoh and his people placed such reliance. In or of infliction the plagues were the death of cattle (the god of which was Apis), boils upon the bodies of the Egyptian (Isis, the goddess of medicine and peace), ubiquitous swarms of flies (Khepri), hail falling from a clear sky and turning to fire (Nut), the legendary plague of locusts (Seth, god of storms and disorders), and what should have been the knife in Pharaoh's heart, continual darkness, (Amon-ra, the mighty sun god). After each Pharaoh momentarily relented but after which he rehardened his heart. Again, with the Israelites remaining in bondage, it was God's play. Unsurprisingly the Creator of not just Egypt but the universe itself was up to the challenge. God Himself now narrates:

> "Thus saith the Lord,
> About midnight will I go out in the land of Egypt:

> And all the firstborn in the land of Egypt shall die, from the firstborn of Pharaoh that sitteth upon his throne, even unto the firstborn of the maidservant that is behind the mill; and all the firstborn of beasts."

The Israelites were to be spared the terror of this tragedy if they painted (or washed) the lintels and door posts of their dwellings with the blood of a newly sacrificed lamb so "... that you may know that the Lord doth put a difference between Israel and the Egyptians." Thus, God's angel of death would pass over the homes of His people, saving them and sparing their destruction. This "Passover" was then ordained to be the yearly Jewish celebratory feast of "Passover," still practiced by today's observant Jewish community as the eight-day feast of Pesach.

The first nine plagues were purely destructive, horrifying calamities which in their aggregate must have turned the mighty land of Egypt into a fouled sewer of death, disease, filth and misery. The tenth, the death of the firstborn, was even worse. On top of what the Egyptians had already experienced now added the sudden, unexpected loss of sons and daughters, and in ancient cultures the firstborn was especially esteemed. So often, though, both scholastically and theologically, the salvation of the Jews and its special avenue has been overlooked. Literally, those whose houses were washed in the blood of the lamb were saved. The true meaning of this, though, was not realized and understood until over a millennium the true Lamb of God, Jesus Christ, came and by His blood the salvation of the obedient, Jew, Egyptian, or any Gentile was secured.

But for the moment all the gods and goddesses of Egypt had been shown to be vacuous nullities. Pharaoh remained a powerful rule, but he apparently had learned the limits of his power. After four hundred thirty years this megalomanic of a ruler (by no means a historically exclusive distinction) was to be the great Pharaoh who finally released the Israelites from bondage. In this, he was a ruler who was in back of his own people, for the Egyptians were in haste to rid themselves of the Israelites for they hoped that their absence and exodus would bring them peace "... for they said, We be all dead men." To employ a modern expression the Egyptians now had such an urgency to rid their land of Israelites that they helped them pack. They gave these long serving slaves material wealth, jewels, gold, and silver, and the Israelites themselves engaged in pillage and "spoiling" Egypt of its wealth, an early example of the economic "justice" of reparations. The great exodus of the Hebrews from Egypt, which for almost numberless reasons, historical, legal, spiritual, etc., remains one of the key points in history had arrived. Yet, for just one final moment let us consider what Moses and the Israelites were leaving behind in Egypt.

This land of the Nile remained a great power and civilization, although its golden age was already behind it at the time of the Exodus, which measurably enhanced its downward spiral. We must be given to make inquiry as to why an omnipotent God followed this course rather than just freeing the Israelites by His Will and Word. Always we must tread lightly when we attempt to discern God's thinking and reasoning, but here much is factually evident. The scriptures, especially those of the Old Testament, provide us many easily discernible reasons.

The signs and wonders of the Ten Plagues and the very definite reality of the emancipation of upwards of one million slaves were subjects, which while sometimes and shamefully forgotten by the Israelites themselves, continued for centuries their service as objects of wonder and awe among many

Gentiles who heard of them, a couple of whom will be referenced in this book. For thousands of years they have believed and taught by God's faithful, although their universal awareness has shown signs of fading though not vanishing, in our rabidly secular age. These timeless wonders, though, are still a joyful beacon of light to all sincere believers, and it is a light which will never dim nor be extinguished.

May we never forget the centrality of God's design to humble and reveal the limitations of the most powerful man on earth, the Egyptian Pharaoh. God's edict at the beginning of the epoch of plagues merits another reference, as He announced to Moses that "... the Egyptians shall know that I am the Lord, when I bringeth forth my hand upon Egypt." The Egyptians found this to be true, but what about their own lord and master Pharaoh. Powerful men and women and the kingdoms, empires, monarchies, even republics and democracies they rule, loathe any challenge or resistance to that power. This is inclusive of men such as Pharaoh and other giants of ancient history such as Alexander the Great or Julius Caesar. It is likewise true of the modern techno-bureaucratic state and its managers and would be monarchs, even though their persona and depth are pale, pastel images of a Pharaoh, Alexander or Caesar. Worldly power hates the source of true power, which God had just shown Pharaoh to be Himself. The state, in whatever form, fears rivals, and Pharaoh knew, although it was not a knowledge of true knowledge, that when Moses and his God confronted him his own power, which to him was absolute, had to be upheld. Instead, God utilized the intransigence, the darkness and the hardness of Pharaoh's heart to defeat him.

Israel was about to be released from over four centuries of slavery for the people had been redeemed from bondage by the actions and love of God. Even more importantly. The Divine ultimate plan of redemption had taken a massive step forward. The far greater exodus from sin to salvation would have its even more awesome moment over one thousand years hence in an overcrowded city nestled in an obscure nation. For the moment, though, all hearts, eyes, and hopes were turned to a people, likely some 600,000 strong which were to be led from Egypt through a harsh land fraught with perils. What would be their fate?

CHAPTER THREE

LEAVING HOME

The act of moving human beings from one locale to another is the very quintessence of the phrase "easier said than done." Any mother in even a small family soon learns that the simplest outing of her beloved family can be an organizational, management and administrative challenge of epic dimensions. The planning, foresight and labor necessary to transport two adults and perhaps two or three children from home to a weekend retreat, be it a hotel or the grandparents' home is somewhat staggering, especially to the neophyte mother and father. Our imagination should now prompt us to consider a force multiplier of from 200,000 to 300,000 to where the small family is now a nation of close to one million souls, only a few of which we even recognize and know by name. With this vast population would come herds of all sorts of livestock, cattle, sheep, goats, etc., personal property and the spoils and detritus of their long-time forced home. The multitude would be of every age from infancy to the extreme aged, and all sorts of physical and health problems would beset vast numbers of them. They had but little food or water, and the excitement of beginning a new trip would soon dissipate into a desert sun.

In some important respects, though, the migration of the Hebrews to a new land was not unique. Among other things history itself is a scenic backdrop to the migration of persons, populations, ethnic groups and nations from one point to another. The Caucasian people of central and western Europe which have had such an influence on history (for good or bad, depending upon one's perspective) largely came from central Asia before migrating to the nations we know as England and France. From the 1500's onward massive numbers of Spaniards, Portuguese and others came westward across the Atlantic and mixed with the indigenous people of South and Central America to form Latin America. In the east Asians crossed the waters across the northern Pacific and became the nation of Japan. The story is told ad infinitum, but the one of the Exodus is unique for a plethora of reasons. This was an immigration, an exodus, but it was more importantly a Divinely sponsored prison break from close to a half millennium of the degradation of slavery.

The movement of such a mass of people eastward is astonishing to contemplate, much less to accomplish. The actual exodus of such numbers must have consumed not days, but weeks, and only one person even knew where they were going. For certain they left Egypt and entered an eastern desert wilderness, but only their leader knew that their first goal was Mount Sinai. The emotional uplift of leaving slavery sent spirits soaring above the Hebrews. Like school children (a term which will become woefully descriptive of them), leaving for a school field trip or the ecstasy of the beginning of summer vacation they were giddy at the prospects of absolute freedom, entirely new lives and the burden of the shackles of slavery becoming a distant memory. But how would they get there? The burning desert across which they trod was absent of the Egyptian slave masters, but so was it lacking just about everything else.

With the passing of each day the coming of the next surely brought the realization that they were engaged in a trek of freedom, but it was across the burning sands and to where and for what purpose? From the Torah's account it is found that when they left their slave quarters in Egypt's eastern Land of Goshen, they went first to a place aptly named Ramses and then generally in a southerly direction to Succoth. At this juncture, though, God did not heed the ancient folk wisdom as well as the laws of physical. The most direct route to Mt. Sinai would have been directly eastward, but the Lord realized that disaster lay there, and nowhere is this better expressed than in Exodus itself:

> "God led them not through the land of the Philistines, although that was near; for God said, Lest peradventure the people repent when they see war, and they return to Egypt."

The Philistines controlled the northerly land routes of the Sinai Peninsula and also much of the western sectors of the Promised Land of Canaan. They were a harsh, crude, fierce and warlike people and would themselves for later centuries become a continual Biblical bete noir for Israel. The Philistines most infamously produced the hulking Goliath (think David and Goliath) and were always a sinister and ferocious enemy. A considerable stretch of the Old Testament is the story of the hostilities, wars and destruction between the two nations until the Philistines were subdued by Israel's most famous king. This was in the future, though, and God knew that his Israelite people were the products of grim, emasculating slavery and had neither the fortitude, the courage or the maturity to stand up to the people. For God so knew His people that He knew that in their hearts they remained slaves. This was an instance when the most direct route would destroy God's plans for His Chosen. The spiritual application not to the Israelites alone should be all too obvious. A novice, a neophyte believer, does not yet possess the spiritual experience and strength which hopefully will mark the believer's more mature character.

So, if the Hebrews took not the more direct northern land route what remained was the southern route, and this meant traversing the Red Sea. This strait of the Indian Ocean separating the continents of Africa and Asia was not a shallow stream to be waded across but rather an enormous barrier over which Moses had no power. Historians, theologians and geographers still argue over the exact location to which the vast horde of Hebrews was led, but for the reader it is sufficient to know that it was somewhere on the western shore of the Red Sea. The Chosen of God were now backed up to the proverbial immovable object, and now the irresistible force was to clasp them in a pincers movement. Neither was truly a force of either man or nature, for this one final scene. Again, God spoke to Moses:

> "Pharaoh will say of the children of Israel, they are entangled in the land, the wilderness hath shut them in
> And I will harden Pharaoh's heart, that he shall follow after them: and I will be honored upon Pharaoh, and upon all his host: that the Egyptians may know that I am the Lord.
> And they did so."

With such a will and His words God ordained the final battle in His clash between Himself and the gods of Egypt. Pharaoh's stone like heart led the mightiest of monarchs to dispatch his great army in pursuit of the Israelites, the time with the purpose of their destruction with Pharaoh's elite forces in the vanguard:

> "And he took six hundred chosen chariots, and all the chariots of Egypt, and captains over every one of them."

Pharaoh's forces finally overtook the Israelites as they were camped upon the western shores of the Red Sea. Ten times the Israelites had been delivered from the scourge of plagues in Egypt, yet when they saw the fiercely driven war chariots driving down upon them, they were petrified with fear, certain of their own destruction and railing against Moses with fearfully threatening and bitterness:

> "Because there were no graves in Egypt, hast thou taken us away to die in the wilderness?'"
>
> Is not this the word that we did tell thee in Egypt, saying,
> Let us alone, that we may serve the Egyptians?
> For it had been better for us to serve the Egyptians than that we should die in the wilderness."

More, much, much more was to come from these emancipated Hebrews, but it must be recounted and noted that every single step of the way, no matter what they had seen or experienced, no matter how miraculous was their delivery from dangerous peril and destruction. Moses, but more importantly, God, had to "prove" Himself to the Israelites. If this generation of Israelites had been given a national motto, as they walked away from the degradation of Egyptian slavery, they should have had emblazoned on banners which they carried "Yes, God, but what have you done for us lately?" God, tested beyond human, but not Divine endurance was about "to do something" for them, a deed the memory of which would never expire. The dialogue for the event's prologue was entrusted to Moses as he spoke to his fellow Israelites:

> "Fear ye not, stand still, and see the salvation of the Lord, which He will show to you today: for the Egyptians whom ye have seen today ye shall see them again no more forever."

"Stand still" is not the easiest admonition to heed, whether it be for ancient Hebrews or modern western people, especially Americans. Many, if not most of us, have been taught from infancy to face problems and difficult situations, to consider possible routes of behavior, and there to be active, to "always" act. It is hard to stand still when engulfed by gloom, worry, fear or terror, but now the Hebrews were given no other choice. Only God, acting through His appointed, Moses, could save them, for the simply possessed none of the wherewithal to save themselves. Militarily, totally lacking armed forces, the Israelites were caught in a pincers movement between an elite force of killers and the immovable object of an arm of the ocean, the Red Sea. The moment and event of God's action would be the single most dramatic scene between the time of Creation and the Advent of Christ. As in a famous cinematic version of the event, Moses stretched out his shepherd's rod, and the waters of the Red Sea parted.

Now, the Hebrews walked across the seabed as dry land, the waters of the sea walls to them on both their right and left hands. How long it took is a matter for historical conjecture, but while crossing the Egyptians were restrained and held back by a pillar of fire. Eventually, though, the pillar was extinguished, and a fierce, capable and brutal Egyptian military force bore down upon the Hebrews. Moses, however, again stretched forth the rod, the waters closed, and all the Egyptian and their horses drowned. The Old Testament's most famous and spectacular miracle had been the final means by which the Israelites had been saved. Now, they were free to go to Mount Sinai and fulfill a major portion of God's plans. Briefly, an aside recognizes that many people, including Pharaoh, scoffed and still do at the idea of the ocean being parted merely by divine will. In contravention to the skepticism, though, may it not be successfully posited that a God who could create an ocean had as well the power to part it?

After four hundred thirty plus years the Israelites truly could revel in the freedom from the Egyptian slave shackles and the egocentricity of their Pharaoh. While they were slaves no longer were they truly free men and women? It took but little of the calendar to provide answers to this question. Moses led his people eastward through the Desert Wilderness of Shur where water was scarce and then into the Wilderness of Sin where the Hebraic chorus was not only about water but how much they missed the food of their old life in Egypt. Moses, at God's behest, was leading this multitude of humanity to their first real goal of Mount Sinai, but what really was he leading. Although the Israelites had been freed by the power of God, Moses was still leading a mass of people who remained slaves, childish slaves, in their hearts. They "believed" in their God, but perhaps that belief could best have given voice if they carried banners emblazoned with the words "Yes, God, but what have You done for me lately?"

The Hebrews for centuries, endless generations, had been subjected to the chains and shackles of slavery, and the ordor of this life had formed and warped their individual and national character. Probably it is impossible for a free person to fully contemplate the effects which slavery has upon a people who have experienced nothing else for as far back as their collective memory recalls. For millennia and especially in antiquity, though, seemingly it was the natural order of things. The Law which God would soon ordain forbade His people from enslaving one another, but the Greeks, Romans, Egyptians, Persians, et al., practiced it as the natural order. Throughout the Middle Ages the Roman Catholic Church frowned upon it, but it survived in modified and softened form as serfdom. It had a rebirth with the discovery of the Americas and was not fully extinguished even in that very Arcadia of modern freedom. America, until the nineteenth century conflagration known as the Civil War.

What must slavery, long lasting generational slavery, done to the character of its victims, in our study the Hebrews? It broke them of individuality, robbed the men of their manhood, reduced women to objects and made all, men and women both, a grotesque form of half human, half work animal, existing only to serve their masters, with Pharaoh at the pinnacle of a very real pyramid. Their individualism and thinking was confined to their own carnal needs, for a slave had no reason to think. His or her job was in the service of the Egyptians and the grandiose building schemes of Pharaoh. Thinking, heritage, ancestry, theology, and so forth were needless luxuries. He was brought up to serve Pharaoh, and his carnal needs, as determined by Pharaoh, would be provided. As for spirituality, it is not opinion that is expressed, but documented fact, that the Hebrews' religion of monotheistic worship of Jehovah, was the thinnest of veneers. The people who left Egypt were God's Chosen, but they soon demonstrated that God was not their Chosen. This was the people that Moses led across the desert wilderness until the nation finally arrived at the base of Mount Sinai.

Some three months since the exodus had elapsed when the Israelites arrived at the base of Mount Sinai, a moderately high mountain at the southern end of what is now called the Sinai Peninsula. It is here that simultaneously two of history's most remarkable stories occurred until finally the stories and their Deities themselves clashed in a great cacophony at the mountain's base. But first, there was a preliminary scene that is often and easily overlooked. God called Moses to come to Him, and on Sinai Moses was given a message:

> "Ye have seen what I did unto the Egyptians, and how I bare you on eagles' wings, and brought you unto Myself.
> Now therefore, if you will obey My voice indeed and keep My covenant, then ye shall be a peculiar treasure unto Me above all people, for all the earth is Mine."

With this monumental message (of which the above is only a portion) came down the mountain and called to himself a group of the Israelite leaders. His message was that God Himself in but three days would come down upon Mount Sinai at which time any who touched even the edge of Sinai would suffer death.

On that third day the mountain was engulfed in thunder, lightning and smoke as the prelude to God's appearing at the peak of Sinai. Moses, and Moses only, went up to meet the Creator of all and listened as God spoke directly to him. What now preceded was a panoply of God's strength, majesty and greatness, beyond the capabilities of even the greatest of writers to express. He commenced with the foundational truth that is forever unshaken and even untouched.

> "Thou shalt have no other gods before Me."

What was delivered to Moses from Heaven were nine more laws, all known collectively then and forever after as the Ten Commandments, the basis of Judaism and later Christian morality. Yet today they remain as affixed in God's moral firmament as they were in the stone tablets in which He chiseled them. Often the Israelites ignored them, flouted them, even mocked them, all to their peril and near total destruction. While we live under the true Deliverer, the Redeemer, Jesus Christ, it remains that any nation or people which ignores them or scoffs at them does so at its dire peril.

Even so, the Ten Commandments was not all that God provided Moses. Two books of the Torah, Exodus and Leviticus, contain detailed chapter after chapter outlining both civil and criminal laws. When completed this Law of Moses far surpassed any other legal code possessed by contemporary nations God pronounced His own benediction upon His work, as He explained to Moses:

> "It is a sign between Me and the children of Israel forever: for in six days the Lord made heaven and earth, and on the seventh day He rested, and was refreshed."

For the moment, though, the people of Israel were not impressed.

Without regard to class, sex or race prolonged slavery, its cruel suffocation of the spirit, does many vile deeds. Among the worst, probably the most malevolent of all, slavery transforms a nation's people from strong men and women to children. The childishness of the Hebrews at the base of Sinai was a wonder still to behold. One of the defining traits of childhood, possessed by every person who ever lived, is impatience. A child measures time by a differently calibrated clock than does a mature adult, and now the childishness of all Israel was to blossom in full flower. Moses "delayed to come down out of the mount," and what little patience the Israelites owned soon crumbled, and the floodwaters of their own destruction were about to engulf them. It is recorded:

> "The people gathered themselves together unto Aaron and said unto him,
> Up, make us gods which shall go before us; for as for this Moses, the man that brought us up out of the land Egypt, we know not what has become of him."

How the mighty have fallen in the esteem of the public. The figure who had sacrificed his own life, desires and comforts to free them, who had been the Divine instrument for ten miracles as noteworthy today as they were three and one-half millennia past had now become just "this man." To the shock and the dismay of God, Moses and believers to follow in the centuries to come the mutinous Israelites found their man in Aaron, the strong right arm of Moses himself. Aaron acceded to the people's fevered desires for folly, and he directed to dispense with all their gold jewelry, much, perhaps most of it pilfered from the Egyptians. From this his skilled hands fashioned the golden calf of lasting infamy which elicited from Aaron the startling proclamation that "these by thy gods, O Israel, which brought thee up out of Egypt." With an aplomb and rebellion that astonishes still in the twenty-first century while Moses was receiving from God the first commandment of the exclusivity of God and the prohibition of graven images, his brother Aaron was fashioning one from precious metal. This deed was many things, and it was truly irony at its most flabbergasting. Still, it was not enough for Aaron. From either fear of the people or a blackening of his own heart Aaron proclaimed the next day a "feast to the Lord." His people responded joyously, and in those words which ring yet today:

> "The people sat down to eat and drink but rose
> up to play."

Whatever control (actually little or none) Aaron may have had for his fellow Israelites had vanished. For a time Moses was unaware of this rebellion, but it had not escaped the eyes of God for he directed Moses:

> "Go, get thee down; for the people which thou
> brought out of the land of Egypt, have corrupted
> themselves."

As the ultimate angry parent the Heavenly Father cautioned Moses to "... let Me alone, that my wrath may wax hot against them, and that I may consume them, for I will make of thee a great nation." Not for the last time did Moses now demonstrate his greatness as a leader and a man for he reminded God of everything that He had done, of the miracles He performed and His promises to Israel. Among men only Moses could have changed God's mind as He "... repented of the evil which he thought to do unto the people." Moses was the supreme example of an intercessor until the Great Intercessor appeared some fourteen centuries later.

For the present, though, Moses faced a scene of degradation, confusion and rebellion which would have defeated almost all mortal men. As he came down, he was met by young Joshua who told Moses of a "... noise of war in the camp."

A panoply of riot, idolatry and perversion met the eyes of Moses when he descended the mountain. He saw all that, and we may but imagine and offer conjecture as to his heart's status when he espied the golden calf. With his anger (which could be fierce) aroused, he broke the tablets of The Ten Commandments. The golden calf itself fell victim to the wrath of Moses as he had it melted down, ground to powder, scattered it upon the Israelites' drinking water and forced them to partake. That was not all. Some three thousand rebels were literally put to the sword, and the mutinous immoral rebellion was squelched. Remaining, though, was a type of confrontation that is woven into the world's history and the fabric of family and society – brother against brother. Moses had shielded his recalcitrant and highly disappointing brother from God's wrath, but Moses himself had a simple obvious question to lay before Aaron:

> "What did this people thee, that thou has brought
> so great a sin upon them?"

Aaron, a man of ability, high intelligence, demonstrated wisdom and courage replied with an answer for the ages, the ages of stupidity and nonsense. He tried to allay his brother's anger with a defense that is little, if any, removed from the trite and banal "boys will be boys," and our people, the Israelites will be foolish. In Aaron's explanation the golden calf was a sort of tertiary deity, a symbol for Moses, who was gone. Then, his answer to Moses concluded with a sentence which will live not only in "infamy" but also incredulity:

> "And I (Aaron) said unto them,
> Whosoever hath any gold, let him break it off, so they gave it to me: then I cast it into the fire and there came out this calf."
> There came out this calf?

This calf, so symbolic of the state of the Israelites (and also of the weakness of Aaron) had two gestation periods before its birth. The obvious, this golden abhorrence which came from the heat of the furnace was physical and could be measured in days and hours. The second gestation period was emotional and had begun at the onset of 430 years of slavery. As has been referenced earlier, slavery is debilitating. Crushing physically, morally and most important spiritually. The calf was the toy of the moment and somehow in the massive childish mindset of the Israelites its mere presentation as the first "float" in a mass national self-degradation of a penitential parade back into Egypt. The concept of yet another pagan idol placating the ferocious wrath of Pharaoh is ludicrous. The whole idea was an evil, but childishly ridiculous fantasy that was worthy of children only, but these children were presumably adults. We in the perch of three thousand plus years later are compelled to conjecture what would their attitude have been if they had known that Pharaoh had planned to massacre them all at the Red Sea before God's miraculous intervention. The Hebrews, neither for the first nor the last time, had refused to accept the hard truth, repeated in many ways throughout the ages, that truly you cannot go home again. Still, if they could not retreat to that supposed den of comfort of Egyptian slavery what were their other national (and dare we say "ethnic") character traits that had led them to childishness at Sinai, open idolatry and rebellion and the continual displeasures of God and the leadership of their fellow Israelite Moses?

The word "murmur" itself has a semi-strange euphony to its pronunciation, yet it is a marvelously descriptive term. The repetitive sound of the word, a double-barreled shot of a syllable, "mur," which in isolation sounds somewhat nonsensical aptly suits the Israelite people which marched away from Egyptian slavery. For what it is worth we offer one of the modern definitions from The Concise Oxford Dictionary of English.

> "Murmur. A subdues expression of discontent."

Murmuring actually commenced in Eden with the first serpentine utterance from Satan, and it has never shown any indication of its subsiding in our modern times. The ancient Israelites, though, can offer a substantial claim to being the premier murmurers of all history. Even while the Israelites were making their way in the wilderness of Sin, even subsequent to their miraculous national rescue in the Red Sea crossing and the previous miraculous emancipation from Egyptian bonds, but before their gathering at Sinai this is as succinct a scriptural description of their moral character as may be found:

> "And the whole congregation of the children of Israel murmured against Moses and Aaron in the wilderness."

Let us apply our focus to a couple of individual words in the quoted sentence, the first being children and the second murmured. Although in this sentence the word "children" apparently is to be interpreted primarily as "Israelite" it is remarkably apropos of the mental and emotional state of the sons and daughters of Israel. Childhood is, or at least should be, an era of golden hues and melodies from those few years of life. It provides strength to a man or woman as that person proceeds through the joys, hardships and vicissitudes of adult life. Piteous is the adult (and they are always extant) whose memories of childhood are nothing but travail, darkness and pain. At the other extreme, and an extreme that has many temptations of increasing allure, is to be ensnared in the trap of making all childhood as golden. It is not, and the scriptures chastise any person or nation that clings to childhood rather than mature. Some fifteen hundred years alter the great apostle Paul summarized God's understanding of childhood and His people's expected growth:

> "When I was a child I spake as a child,
> I understood as a child, I thought as a child: but
> when I became a man I put away childish things."

The Israelites, massive though they were in numbers, which Moses led from Egypt, need put away childish things. We have already spoken of their impatience but how often and for decades to come would their natural stumbling of character growth be demonstrated by continual murmuring or complaining.

A strong element of childhood, whether we remember it this way of not, is the concept of complaining, done by all children, good and bad. Spanning all cultures and generations is the child who can never be satisfied, except by momentary thrills, and whose desires and whims must be continuously placated. Israel is the days of Moses was composed of a large nation of such people, by chronology adults but by emotion children. God was not fooled, for He always knew that it really was neither Moses nor Aaron against whom they murmured, but God himself. The signature stamp of both a spoiled, petulant child and the Israelites led by Moses is their impossibility of being satisfied except for that brief wistful moment or two of exhilaration from obtaining the whim of the moment. Already, against impossible odds they had freed from Egyptian slavery, been saved from the horrors and demise brought by the plagues, led across an unknown desert wilderness, and provided food and water. No surprise that God Himself called them a "stiff necked" people.

A reference was made previously to the statement that at the foot of Mount Sinai and upon making the infamous golden calf the Israelites "rose up to play." Play is one of the dearer parts of life, hopefully a large component of one's childhood and its memories, and not a Biblical word ever condemns nor discourages play for an adult. Surely, this work does not seek to disparage play, fun and games, amusement, entertainment or whatever other word may be applied. The "play" of the Israelites (or at least some of them) after their impatience at Moses's "delay" had devolved into something different. Many of these Hebrews could no longer maintain any façade of worshipping God and eschewing paganism. Exodus records that they had thrown off all pretense and resorted to an almost primordial form of heathenism, including nakedness, perversion and most abhorrent, human sacrifice. This was their play, and it is hardly to be questioned that the patience of the Almighty was broken, and he condemned some 3,000 of them with additional plans for retribution. None of this, neither the childishness nor the moral debauchery at Sinai, was done in a vacuum, for it was a natural outgrowth of other vices that appeared to be almost endemic among the Israelites.

Let us express a monumental understatement and posit that all human beings and all sentient creatures are concerned about food and water. The concern is daily, and at times is desperate. So were the Hebrews, this enormous body of humanity that had made its exodus from Egypt, and certainly no sin attached to such a concern. What provisions they had were soon depleted, and now this mass of humanity, approaching one million in number, began to wonder from whence would come the daily sustenance of life. Our narrative has already noted the Divinely provided water and the food in the miraculous regular appearance of a substance called "manna," a term which retains a certain currency seen in modern English. The provision of the manna and the reaction of the Israelite people countenances a deeper look. Miraculously, water was Divinely provided by God, enough for the population of a fairly large modern metropolis and provided from the hot, dry environs of the desert. As for food while man does not live by bread along still, he must have bread to survive. Supposedly, the Israelites knew that they were on a journey to serve and worship God, but how can they or any people be castigated for desiring the basics of life? They were hungry and fearful, but the God of Heaven was not deaf nor hardened to their concerns. Daily He miraculously provided them bread in the form of manna, a honied wafer like food which sustained them. The satisfaction of the Hebrews, though, had but a short life span. Manna was life sustaining to be sure, but it was boring and soon became monotonous by its ubiquity. The Israelites wanted variety, and again (as if they would ever stop) began to murmur and complain. Again, though, God the Divine ever patient Father heard their cry and through Moses He spoke:

> "(T)he Lord shall give you in the evening flesh to eat, and in the morning bread to the full, for that the Lord heareth your murmurings which you murmur against Him: and what are we? Your murmurings are not against us, but against the Lord."

God was true to His promise, and in the evening, quails were provided, but the daily ration of bread in the morning would in no way subside. Let it be injected here with but a touch of irony and humor that the Creator Himself was the master nutritionist, providing a balanced diet of carbohydrates and protein with even a bit of sweetener tossed into the menu. It was a good, solid plentiful diet and well that it was, for the "children of Israel did eat manna forty years, until they came to a land inhabited." For many of the fugitives from Egypt even this was not enough, as they mournfully expressed;

> "We remember the field which we did not eat in Egypt freely; the cucumbers and the melons, and the leeks, and the onions, and the garlic."

Many then remembered Egypt as a land of the gourmand's fanciful delight, and conveniently the prime characteristic of their national sojourn had slipped the traces of the memory – abject slavery. These refugees of Egypt were living proof of a famous Shakespearean quote that "... security is mortal's chiefest enemy." Their thoughts and words also laid bare an ever ripening but rarely examined human emotion, that of nostalgia.

Our text will dispense with a dictionary definition of "nostalgia," for among other things it is a term and an emotion that is so heartfelt and individualized that its meaning and definitions are practically equal to the population totals themselves. At a minimum it is a longing for the past, or perhaps more to the point the past as the person so recalls. It is far from evil, and it is the rare, even piteous person who does not have fond, even golden hued memories of childhood, of boyhood, girlhood, youth, parents, siblings and friends and the multitude of promises and pleasures that derive from being young. Not as commonly recalled are the hurt feelings, the insecurities and depending upon the person the many fears that are attendant to youth. At a certain age we long for freedom and independence while still enjoying the security of home, often forgetting that we were chafing under the authority, even if just and lacking abuse, of our parents.

Nostalgia for the past can easily become an entrapment and often can be modified and ameliorated only by a healthy dose of the remembrance of realism. Whatever our age and circumstances, each person and each nation is beset with problems. The nostalgic warmth and happy glow of a joyous time and occasion can be visited mentally from time to time, but it should not and cannot serve as a roadblock for our future travels. For the Israelites it was a nostalgia for security, and this nation along believes the truism that humanity seeks freedom. Freedom was and so remains in "free" countries deeply subordinate to the desire for physical comfort and security. For the Israelites it impeded and eventually halted the progress of the emancipated slaves for the Promised Land of freedom, responsibility, and prosperity. For decades God and Moses had to deal with this attitude until this generation of slaves faded from the scene.

So this was the "nation" of Israel which surrounded the Holy Mountain of Sinai while Moses ascended it heights to confer with God Himself and receive the Law by which His people would live. An inchoate mass of humanity, banded together only by the basic of human traits and desires, many if not most proving to be bad, it was an unpleasant, often gruesomely repugnant amalgam of childishness, impatience, idolatry, a silly, trivialized nostalgia and rebellion which broke through the thinnest veneer of propriety and Godliness. This was God's chosen nation, His chosen people, who had gathered at the base of Sinai and who would succeed in putrefying this most holy occasion in the world's history. But what of their leader, Moses? At best he was reluctant to answer God's clarion call to leadership, and in its earliest phase he himself had almost brushed with the concept of rebellion. Before we examine at length the Moses who descended Mount Sinai with the Law let us spare a glance into the character of the Moses who had ascended the mount.

Moses at Mid-Career

As the scriptures from Exodus, penned by Moses himself, are clear from the time of his confrontation with Pharaoh, through the days of the Ten Plagues, the exodus and the parting of the Red Sea, Moses gave meaning to the term "busy" that has yet to be surpassed or even equaled some three- and one-half millennia later. He had time for little but being God's instrument and the shepherd and father to his infant (in more ones than one) nation. With an apparent momentary respite from his labors on the route to Sinai he was reunited with his wife Zipporah, his two sons Gershom and Eleazar along with Moses's father-in-law, a man named Jethro, himself a figure of substance being the sheik of Medran. Jethro was a good man with a good relationship with his son in law Moses (such never being an automatically elementary task). He himself was a worshipper of the God of Moses, and Jethro had not only affinity and admiration for Moses but personal concern as well.

On the second day of Jethro's visit he accompanied Moses as his son in law judged the people from "morning unto the evening." Moses, the leader of almost a million-person group sat as a one-man judiciary from daylight to dark, and Jethro was so aghast he said:

> "What is tis thing that thou doest to the people?
> Why sittest thou thyself alone, and all the people
> stand by thee from morning to even?"

Moses's answer was respectful but succinct as he explained to his father-in-law "Because the people come unto me to inquire of God."

In the late twentieth century a term was coined to describe persons who are self-driven, exceptionally hard-working and conscientious, attentive to their duties, needful of little or no supervision and goal oriented to an apogee that many cannot comprehend. This person is said to have a "type A personality." If the phrase had been current in Old Testament times Moses may have rightly claimed to be the Old Book's premier example. Jethro recognized the folly and danger inherent in Moses's actions of a fully defined committed and defined Type A personality, the inability to delegate authority. He told his son-in-law that what he was doing was "not good." It was not good for Moses, and it was not good for the Israelite people.

It is one thing to criticize and condemn, but quite another to advise and constructively suggest, the latter course being the one followed by Jethro. He advised Moses to find good men, wise men and appoint them as elders and judges of the people, providing thus for what modern lawyers would call a lower court system. Moses, always the wisest, most conciliatory and modest of men acceded to Jethro's advice, and a portion of the enormous burden which always weighed on Moses was eased. He thus had a council of advisors for the endless stream of problems and required arbitrations and decisions as well as a system that would relieve him of some, if not many or most, minor conflicts. Certainly Moses needed this relief, for the collection of problems, endless murmurings and even outright rebellions had not stopped and neither did the future hold a date for their cessation.

When Moses returned down the slopes of Sinai, as our text has already related, in an almost literal sense all hell had broken loose. His temper, always a force close to the surface, was ignited, and if ever a man had title to justification for righteous anger. Yes, the rebellion was crushed, its core leaders and adherents executed and the Divine restoration of the tablets a fact, but Israel and Moses had passed a watershed. Yes, Moses remained a leader, revered and respected but also the Torah is not hesitant in its revelation of a lurking adversarial relationship between Moses and the Israelites. God had assigned him a task which was to be his life's work, one so heavy with burdens that few other men could even be remotely considered for his role. He did not want it, and already this portion of his life had borne witness to the enormity of the burdens he bore. It is only normal to wonder if Moses knew that he was still at their beginning.

CHAPTER FOUR

THE SCHOOLMASTER

From its birth it has been known by so many names, the Law of Moses, the Mosaical Law, The Ten Commandments, simply "Moses," but as the generations passed among the Israelites, later more commonly referenced as the Jews, it was simply "the Law." This great book of principles, tenets, reasons and regulations certainly set the Israelites apart from other nations, but it was neither the sole nor really even the most important differential. The famed Ten Commandments are the statutes of great density and length which followed, so carefully, intricately and thoroughly set forth in a great section of the Book of Exodus and almost the entirety of the Book of Leviticus are capable of immediate and quick understanding, but their deepest and truest undertaking requires a lifetime, and then some. The Almighty, meticulous and orderly as always, arranged His commandments, the first five being humanity's obligations to God and the second the duties and fealties which all men and women owe to each other. Remarkably, the Ten Commandments themselves contain little that mankind did not already know. The author is deeply aware that the tabulation and revelation of what lawyers typically call "black letter" law is usually tedious, boring and devoid of any sustained interest. Nonetheless due to their centrality to our story and their ever-living foundational importance to the Israelites and all civilization we make an exception and offer them, familiar as they are, in the order received by Moses:

1. Thou shalt have no other gods before Me.
2. Thou shalt not make unto thee any graven image, or any likeness of anything that is in heaven above, or that is in the earth beneath, or that is under the earth.
3. Thou shalt not take unto thee the name of the Lord thy God in vain.
4. Remember the Sabbath day, to keep it holy.
5. Honor thy father and thy mother that thy days may be long upon the earth.
6. Thou shalt not kill.
7. Thou shalt not commit adultery.
8. Thou shalt not steal.
9. Thou shalt not bear false witness against thy neighbor.
10. Thou shalt not covet (anything) that is thy neighbor's.

With honesty and openness it must be conceded that much of these commandments was likewise contained in many other ancient legal systems, naturally including those of the pagans, probably most famously in the Code of Hammurabi of the Babylonians. Neither, though, should this be surprising to any observer, though, since these Ten Commandments are basically a codification of what mankind already knew and had known since his fall in the Garden. Because all since Adam have lived under the curse of death it is difficult to comprehend that sparkling pristine time and environment in which God's creation, and its pinnacle, man, lived in a state of innocence. With his crash from Edenic tranquility and bliss man became immersed in that world where, in the phraseology of Genesis, he now had the knowledge of good and evil, whether or not it had been transcribed upon stone tablets. When humanity had fallen it needed no written code to know, to sense, to feel, that it was wrong, horribly wrong, to murder a fellow human, to steal from him that which was his and to shrug off the Deity who created him. The knowledge was in-born, and ever since what became the darkness of Eden, men and women had known of the nature of evil and their propensity to follow its allure. Certainly ancient man, even if crude, primitive and illiterate, knew the wrong of thievery, that pilfering a co-worker's farming implement or a fellow hunter's bow, and arrow was not only a forbidden wrong but that the repercussions and retribution for such an act could be swift, violent or even deadly. Even such a commandment as the fourth, keeping the Sabbath, possessed an inborn inheritance. God Himself rested from His six-day labor of the Creation, and He knew that His creation required a day of rest from labor. Man has always known this, although large segments of modern humanity, especially in the western world, seems driven to make each week one of seven days, each chock full of the "busy mess" of frenetically work and living.

In the main, then, the Israelites, presumably or putatively the most morally cognizant and advanced of ancient people, were told little of what they did not already know when Moses gave them the law. While he was receiving the Law from the Finger of God Himself, though, His own Chosen, or at least a significant section thereof, was joyously engaged in smashing each law. The question is obvious, then, and it concerns the reason for a written codification of the commands and precepts of God if His people knew them already. Men and women should always try to tread carefully into the territory of the reasons why the Almighty has acted as He does, and we will be no exception. A blessing is found in the scriptures, though, and particularly not in the Old but in the New Testament, which did not follow until the passage of some fifteen hundred years. Already the narrative has revealed that the Hebrew slaves who made the exodus from Egypt were children, and as the text will reveal the childishness did not easily, if ever, abate. They, like all children, needed rules and the knowledge of consequences, even penalties, if those rules were not heeded. Spiritually, and we believe the continuing metaphor is strong enough to bear this symbolism, they were kindergarteners, who petulantly, even violently resisted any Divine restraints upon their conduct. They were like children throwing a continuous tantrum, and God Himself readily availed Himself of such descriptive terms. But int his world, the Israelites, as do we all, exit its mortal hold upon us by death. The generation of the Exodus, the nation of Israel and the successor truncated land of Judah (or Judea) all had their place in the sun before vanishing. Notwithstanding any claims of the modern state of Israel, the Chosen people and their land of Israel had been vanquished (many items actually) and had been permanently subsumed by other nations at the close of the scriptures. Most assuredly the Law which Moses brought down the slopes of Sinai was valuable, even essential, but only for a time. Fifteen centuries later it was early Christianity's most prominent herald, the apostle Paul who wrote to his fellow Christians:

> "Wherefore the law was made schoolmaster to bring us unto Christ, that we might be justified by faith.
> For after that faith is come, we are no longer under a schoolmaster."

The truly educated person is always striving for a goal, and God, its author, knew that the Low of Moses alone was not intended as a permanent fixture, an ever-lit lamp to guide His people to salvation. The word "schoolmaster" in its most literal rendering is "child leader," and such exactly was the Mosaical Law, a beautiful, precise mechanism and guide to salvation in the person of Jesus Christ alone.

The Israelites (and their numbers were substantial) who obeyed God and followed the Law were great beneficiaries of the Law, its order and precepts, but the true recipient of its blessing, or more properly its one great blessing, Christ, would be the Christian.

Still, what of the still present, the extant Law of Moses, for the Israelites who would now be living under its precepts and principles? Were the Ten Commandments, which to the world then and now, is capable of reduction to a set of homilies, all there was to the Law of Moses? Most emphatically, no. To employ modern Anglo-American legal terminology, the Ten Commandments was the newly transcribed constitution for the Israelites. What followed were the statutes, the statutory law that guided daily life. The Law itself comprises a large swath of the book of Exodus, almost all of Leviticus and great portions of Numbers and Deuteronomy. Its substance reflects the intentions of a God who wishes to provide everything for His people, be it physical, emotional and especially spiritual. Little aspect of life's purposes and the details of daily living are neglected. Since our perspective is from what we call modern let us first categorize the Law into two sections, a division still employed today, that of the civil and the criminal.

Thankfully since most men and women in any (but not all) societies are not criminals the civil aspect of the Law of Moses should acquire our first review. The Law was more civil than it was criminal. The space available in a work such as the present one affords an opportunity only to discuss its precepts, edicts and judgments in the most summary fashion. Beneath it all and thoroughly imbued in every law was a desire to bring the people closer to God, His ideas of justice and His way of thinking. Rather than attempt a general survey of countless laws and concepts likely the best method of revealing God's thinking on one particular facet of life and the law, and that is restitution for harm and injuries suffered. Restitution is a highly and remarkably defined word, given different meanings in different times and in a vast assortment of societies and legal systems. Even modern, scholarly dictionaries, themselves the products of fine pedigrees of learning have multiple definitions, sometimes similar, quite often with distinctions of meaning. One dictionary consulted succinctly defines the word as "reparation for an injury."

So much of civil law, whether overtly expressed, is founded upon the principle of reparation for an injury. A nation's, a state's, a court's, and most importantly an individual's attitude towards the breadth and extent of those reparations is so defining of it or his/her character. God in His Law recognized that His people would suffer injuries from others, be it intentional, by negligence or through the fault of no one to do. What was the aggrieved party to do imminent of injury and the loss of all or a portion of his life and/or money and property? This is a conundrum which is at the heart of all legal systems and likewise is an element of vexatious controversy to them all. On one extreme is the attitude, seemingly inherent in fallen human beings, is that "I am entitled to whatever I can get without limitation." It is nothing new, and to some degree has permeated like a toxin our own modern legal system. Its most onerous manifestation is the concept of "punitive damages," which bypasses the limiting ruins of just restitution and allows the aggrieved person to receive anything and everything he can from the one who has wronged him. The 'punitive" aspect is to punish him. A fair person and most especially a Christian, and in point of specific fact in the Mosaical Law an observant Israelite, should recognize this is anathema and abhorrent to God's thinking.

Most assuredly economically and financially it was a far different time when Moses received the Law from God, but the underlying reasons and morality of God's thinking luminously shines through the centuries. An example of God's thinking, tough, the specific situation is remote from modern urbanized humanity is found soon after the issuance of the Tenn Commandments:

> "If a man shall open a pit, or if man shall dig a pit, and not cover it, and an ox or donkey fall therein,
> The owner of the pet shall make it good, and give money unto the owner of them: and the dead beast shall be his."

Then, demonstrating He and His Law recognized gradations of conduct and liability in the actions of men this principle is followed by another:

> "If a man shall steal an ox, or a sheep, and kill it, or sell it; he shall restore five oxen for an ox and four sheep for a sheep."

Theft, intentional stealing, is far worse than mere negligence, and its penalties should be greater, although not even then unlimited.

The Mosaic Law continued throughout four books of the Torah, each statute, each regulation, each edict, being an expression of the Creator's concept of justice, punishment, but strictly limited and prescribed where needed, proportionality, fairness and above all mercy.

Regarding mercy we must perceive the criminal side of the Law but not without first mentioning what was and what became uniquely dear and important to the Hebrews, its religious aspect. It is in this realm that the Law of Moses becomes most precise and specific, and upon which the Israelites from time to time continued to construct ever complicated statutes, rules and regulations of every aspect of a person's life. The Book of Leviticus is particularly and specifically concerned with the establishment of religious practices, Sabbath observances, the identity, and duties of the priesthood, the relationship(s) of the priests to God and to man and the necessity of having to deal with the ubiquitous presence of evil and sin, even among God's chosen Israelites. Animal sacrifices, the nature and extent of atonement for sin, duties of the priests and of the people in general are covered in exquisitely crafted detail. Explicitly minute details were given regarding animal sacrifice, the "rituals" of religion and even elaborate dietary guides and restrictions, many of which are as viable today as then. The Sabbath, that final day of the week reserved for rest, Saturday to us, was discussed and regulated at length showing that God was seriously interested in His people resting at least one day each week.

Modern twenty-first century people when they think of the ancient Law of Moses (admittedly a quite rare occurrence) conjure images of an angry Moses as surrogate for his angry God. Legions of long-bearded prophets breathing the proverbial fire and brimstone and inevitably the mantra of "an eye for an eye, a tooth for a tooth" as a symbolic shibboleth for God's approval of some amorphous concept of "Old Testament justice." In dramas, documentaries, works of fiction (quite fictional) it will be uttered by a man or woman who is at a minimum half mad for vengeance for a wrong which has been suffered. The clear implication is that the God of the Old Book delighted not in justice but in retributory vengeance wherein the evildoer suffered without mercy. Actually in reality nothing could be further from the truth, the will of God, then such a fantastic assertion. Most certainly the phraseology, the legal dictate and a certain quintessence of God's attitude towards justice is found in the phrase, perhaps with the singular exception of the Ten Commandments themselves the most famous and quoted portion of the Law, issued first in Exodus as:

> "Eye for eye, tooth for tooth, hand for hand, foot for foot."

In total contravention to several millennia's beliefs that this is an unchecked Divine approval for rampant and bloody vengeance it is more to be interpreted in light of the entirety of the Mosaical Law and God's own character as a guide for reciprocal justice. The blood vengeance of antiquity was anathema to God, a reality whereby many lives, entire families, and in extreme instances whole communities eradicated to appease the vengeful bloodlust excited by the deaths of one person only. "Eye for an eye" fit consistently, perfects even perfectly with the precepts of God's civil law. No man or woman injured would go without recompense for an injury suffered, but neither would they reap an underserved windfall. Permeating much of the Law was a principle later embodied in English common law of making whole" for the suffering of injury, damage or loss.

For an unspecified time this new nation of Israel was to be a theocracy, with one religion and one God only recognized. The governing instrument was the Law of Moses, unlike other legal code or system governing any other land on earth. It was quite lengthy, complex, though certainly not incomprehensible, and made certain demands upon the Hebrew people. Yes, it was burdensome, and the later New Testament referenced it as a "yoke" which burdened the necks of the people. Its later history, as our text will partially disclose, was perilous, calamitous and often destructive. Much of the time it was ignored, at one point even lost and often almost entirely co-opted for the benefit of its clerisy, the priesthood (a not uncommon fate for any religion). In its last days of efficacy, especially into the early days of the New Testament it had become so weighted with tradition, self-serving interpretations by the self-appointed guardians of "true" religion, the scribes, Pharisees and Sadducees that the weight was crushing the people.

But perhaps we are getting ahead of the story. When Moses descended Sinai, he came into a raucous playground of adults who had devolved into children. This generation of newly freed Israelites truly needed the schoolmaster the child leader, of the Law of Moses to lead them down the path ordained for them by God. Would this generation be up to the challenge?

CHAPTER FIVE

A PATIENT GOD, AN EXASPERATED LEADER AND A DISCONTENTED PEOPLE

As he descended the slope of Sinai the steps of Moses may have been both heavier and lighter than when he ascended the mount weeks earlier. Lighter in the sense that his direct meeting with the Creator had gone so well with this receiving both God's personal blessings and the law for His people. Still, as serious a man who ever lived Moses recognized that his own personal duties and burdens had not decreased and would, in fact, intensify as the decades of his very long life progressed. Until the day he passed from this terrestrial orb some forty years later Moses would rise to no sun that did not illuminate his own enormous panoply of responsibilities as the leader of Israel. Now, though, by Good's intervention, ordination and personal authorship Moses had a written, transcribed law by which he and all Israelites could be ruled. As the previous chapter discussed the Law was much more than the Ten Commandments, but it was the latter that was the basis of Hebrew law and life and for that matter the tableau for any legal and moral system that makes even a pretense at civilization. On two stone tablets, written by the Finger of God Himself, Moses carried the original, The Ten Commandments which would guide Israel and which they would forever cherish. But, really, not for long.

With each step down the mountain the deservedly praised and heralded Laws of Moses suffered a lessening of its "lifespan." No, certainly not the Law itself and its many sections and subject matters but rather its physical representation which Moses carried in his hands. Literally, at the moments when Moses was receiving the Law the Israelites were doing their very best to destroy it. Our narrative, of course, has referred to the rebellion and Bacchalian celebrations at the foot of Sinai, wherein much of Israel declared its independence from God. The sounds of the rebellion became increasingly noticeable, even at a distance until young Joshua met Moses on his descent and told his leader that "… there is a noise of war in the camp." Moses, older, more seasoned and more attuned to the people he led, reflexively knew that it was not war which was being heard but instead:

> "And it came to pass as soon as Moses came nigh unto the camp, that he saw the calf, and the dancing: and Moses's anger waxed hot, and he cast the tables out of his hands, and break them before the mount."

Thus, the "lifespan" of the Ten Commandments was shockingly brief, or was this really so? What was being destroyed was not a couple of stone tablets but rather Moses's trust in his fellow Israelites. More importantly, the events at the base of Sinai enkindled an anger in God that did not easily or readily abate. Perhaps more importantly, while God's love for Israel remained, the bonds of trust were broken, and in the future, even at the best of times, were tenuous. So what really had Israel done?

The Israelites had crossed that line which always attracted God's attention, the notice of an extraordinarily patient God but one who would not abide outright rebellion. God, that God of Moses and of the patriarchs before him, Abraham, Isaac and Jacob, simply did not fit the template of the deities that they had begun to make, grotesqueries such as the golden calf. Neither did His single, straight forward morality of the Ten Commandments mesh at all with the hedonistic joys of the false idols and gods which they were fashioning. This early rebellion of the Israelites was a portent of the dark and dreary days to come. A feast celebration to a pagan deity in antiquity is better imagined than described, but we may assert with some confidence that it included among its macabre run human sacrifice and pagan fertility rites. It was rebellion, hedonism and may it be averred Satanism at its worst, all while Moses was receiving the Law directly from God. Naturally, the situation was beyond combustible, and the decadent and rebellious Israelites were about to discover that Moses, later described scripturally as the "meekest of men" also possessed a temper of the first order. His confrontation with his brother Aaron has been reviewed already, but Moses's fury, both individually and as God's voice was ready to shatter all before it. We have the old terminology of the King James Scriptures to thank for a magnificently descriptive rendition of Moses's reaction upon seeing the calf and the adjunctive behavior of the rebels:

> "Moses's anger waxed hot, and he cast the tables out of his hands, and brake them before the Mount."

The physical representation of the law's existence was thus measured by the short span of minutes as Moses had come down. Certainly, though, the Law of God is not confined to carved stone tablets, and the Divine aim was God's desire to ultimately write it upon the hearts of His children. For the moment, though, certain of His children were overdue for punishment. The God of Israel, far more merciful than any or all of His own creation, could be just as impactful in His meting out the full measure of His retributive justice:

> "And (Moses) took the calf which they had made, and burnt it in the fire, and ground it into powder and strewed it upon the water, and made the children of Israel drink."

In a very literal and lasting manner the Israelites would remember with literal bitterness this early nadir of their rebellion. For some three thousand of them, though, their memories would be short circuited as God had them killed for their actions. The Israelites most certainly would remember the Satanic bent of their rebellion, God's reaction and the harsh punishment suffered. Time, as described in the coming narrative, would demonstrate whether they netted any profit from this episode.

In the meantime, Israel, more than ever, needed a strong firm hand, direction and guidance, and it could come only from Moses, the man through whom God acted. The Law now lay literally in broken shards at the base of Mount Sinai, and the next move was given to and by God.

Originally God's anger towards Israel was so fierce that He told Moses literally to leave Him alone while He determined what the next direction would be. God's impulsive desire (and yes, apparently even God has impulses) was to change His longstanding plans of bringing salvation and redemption to humanity through the lineage of Abraham, Isaac and Israel (nee Jacob) and recircuit His grace through the descendants of Moses. The latter, though, Israel needed governing, and what better instrument than the original Law itself. So again Moses ascended Sinai and received a new copy of the same Ten Commandments from the same Lord. This was not all the great prophet and leader received from God. The new tablets were not handed to Moses as a day's assignment and certainly not without Divine majesty. With Moses once again upon the sacred ground of Sinai:

> "(T)he Lord descended in the cloud and stood with him there, and proclaimed the name of the Lord.
> And the Lord passed by before (Moses) and proclaimed,
> The Lord, the Lord God, merciful and gracious, longsuffering and abundant in goodness and truth."

Little could Moses have realized the prophetic nature of what God related to him next. He explained to Moses that God's real nature and desire was patience ("longsuffering" as God termed it) and mercy, but "by no means (could this) clear the guilty." The Law which Moses was receiving from Good would temporarily "handle" sin, save His people from sin's natural consequences, but to be "cleared" of sin would require the coming of the Son of God some fourteen centuries later.

Again, God renewed His covenant with Israel and promised His Chosen His care, Divine goodness and mercy and His continual solicitous care. As always, the thoughts and plans of the Almighty were far advance of even His own "followers." The Israelites had not been rescued from Egyptian bondage, protected in a journey through desert sands merely to linger at Mount Sinai or wander aimlessly in the desert. They were present for a purpose, and it was God's purpose that they take the Promised Land as their own. Egypt held Israel for over four centuries, but to employ a jarringly modern idiom Egypt was now in the rearview mirror. The great land and its civilization was to the west, and Israel's eyes were to be to the east to that Promised Land, a small slice of territory on the eastern Mediterranean coast. The promised new home of the Israelites was not a prefabricated paradise of verdant valleys, rich farmlands and prosperous cities wherein dwelled multitudes of people to greet them with open arms. Actually, it was generously populated by many groups of nationalities and people, most of whom would come to hate the Israelites with a passion as intense, if not more so, in the twenty-first century A.D. as it was fourteen hundred years before the birth of Christ. Many different peoples inhabited this small area, a little enclave of land which has proven to be the most historic, famous, volatile and explosive in all history. So many people with so many names, the Hittites, the Jebusites, the Amorites, the Perizzites, the Amalekites and most famously, or perhaps infamously, the Canaanites. Literally, the Bible and history records dozens of other groups, some large, some small, appearing for a while and then fading from historical record. The ethnological composition and history of these peoples intertwine and overlap, and none are "pure" nationalities. Most, just like the Israelites, were Semitic in heritage, but by far the most dominant were the Canaanites, who for centuries were the great bete noiré of Israel. After all, it was the land of Canaan. These people became so prominent in the Old Testament, and God devoted much attention and instruction about how Israel was to deal with them. It began here on Sinai as God taught Moses.

The Canaanites

Just as it is impossible to tell the story of the nation of Israel, its enslavement and emancipation without hearing reference to Egypt it is as difficult to understand Israel's development without a strong infusion about the people and the nation the Hebrews would encounter in their conquest of the Promised Land. These are the Canaanites, a people and civilization that while certainly not forgotten, perhaps has seen the imprint of its importance fade a bit in recent generations. Once again (and hopefully for the final time) the reader is reminded that the term Canaanite will often be employed to represent the entirety of the population encountered by Israel in its move into the Promised Land.

The great story of what has been called Western Civilization generally has been founded upon two great ancient civilizations, Greece and Rome. Judaism and the Christian faithful generally add Israel and the Jewish culture to this foundation. Almost always lacking in an etymological discussion of the development of our culture and civilization is reference to the Canaanite culture. While certainly not of the value and influence of Greece, Rome and Israel this ancient people could boast great and lasting accomplishments. For example, the Canaanites, primarily through their Phoenician and later Carthaginian descendants were, even more so than the fabled Greeks, the great maritime sailors and commercial developers of western antiquity. They proved to be fine architects and developed their own cities, well-built and strongly fortified. The Canaanites were among the first to alloy metals and because of this practical skill their weapons and weapons delivery systems surpassed those of almost all their enemies. For our purposes and for brevity's sake our eye shall focus upon two fields in which their leadership must be and was in fact supreme.

The first of these great accomplishments was that of the alphabet. Almost all (but not all) our European languages, whether Latin or Germanic or otherwise, are based upon the Latin alphabet, developed by the Romans and to this day marvelously, almost miraculously, flexible and supple in its allowance, even encouragement, of new words and phrases. The Canaanite (later often more commonly referenced as the Phoenician alphabet) was a miscellany of letters, hieroglyphs and symbols and is a brilliant example of the creative genius and intelligence of the Canaanite people. Quite simply, the Canaanites invented the alphabet, yet this was not all they invented.

No people, whether in antiquity, the Middle Ages, modern or post-modern times, east or west, was ever as creative in the creation of god and goddesses as the Canaanites. Historians, archaeologists and others continually add newly discovered deities to the pantheon of Canaanite gods and goddesses. Each god seemed to be a specialist, responsible for only one portion of life, but all served under a mysterious far-removed figure named El, described as a very old man, and sporting a long white beard. El was so removed that the pantheon of deities was actually ruled by his son, that most infamous of all pagan gods, Baal. Likely the second most notorious god in the Canaanite pantheon was Moloch, a being whose hunger was satisfied only by the abomination of child sacrifice. The Canaanites created their gods and goddesses with an easy free will, and no scholar could begin to list them all. Without delving into prurience, though, let it be recognized that the Canaanites had a special proclivity to representing every divine and human act as an expression of not just sexual activity, but rather perversion, sadism and masochism were celebrated and ubiquitous.

Unsurprisingly, such a people as the Canaanites, accomplished, dynamic and with a vicious, almost predatory Satanic desire for human corruption did not escape the notice of God. Back to Sinai and Moses's return to receive the new tablets of the Law God was adamant in His instructions for the Israelites as their time for contact with the Canaanites appeared to be looming:

> "Take heed to thyself, lest thou make a covenant with the inhabitants of the land whither thou goest, let it be a snare in the midst of thee:
> But ye shall destroy their altars, break their images, and cut down their groves."

Hopefully, it is not to trivialize when we make ourselves mindful of a common example of parents and children. Any wise and decent mother or father is very careful about who their children take as companions and friends, not necessarily from any sense of superiority or snobbishness but for fear that their children will be corrupted. Above all fathers God had reason to fear the corruptive immoral influence of the Canaanites. His ultimate fear He expressed to Moses:

> "And thou (Israel) take of their daughters unto they sons, and their daughters go whoring after

> their gods, and make thy sons go whoring after their gods.
>
> Thou shalt make thee no molten gods."

It is ludicrous to import to the Creator of all people, all races, all nationalities, any hint of racism or xenophobia. He fashioned the Canaanites as He did the Israelites, both of Semitic ancestry and likely quite similar in basic physical appearance. God's warning about intermingling of Israel with the Canaanites was not based upon His fear, His apprehension, His worry and certainly not upon a factor as essentiality minimal as a different ethnological identity between Israel and Canaan. It was founded upon the Almighty's Divine knowledge of what He foresaw as certain to happen. The Canaanites would intermarry, intermingle, assert themselves into daily Israelite life and eventually destroy God's special Chosen. In the main, as knows anyone familiar with their history, the Israelites ignored God, and along with other pagan nations which entered the picture eventually destroyed all of Israel, save for a small remnant. Indeed generations of Israelites went "whoring" after false gods and displaced and in many noteworthy instances essentially declared war against their one true God.

It is often believed and falsely quoted that somewhere in the New Testament is emblazoned the quotation of "evil companions corrupt good morals." The exactitude of the statement is missing, but the principle permeates both Testaments. A common belief among God's faithful is that His disciples (now Christians) can influence limitless numbers of the worldly to lead Godly, faithful lives. Yes, it was the Savior Himself who stated that "... a little leaven leaveneth the whole lump." The influence of the good upon the bad should never be denied nor even mocked, but neither should the deleterious influence of the evil upon the virtuous ever be underestimated. God knew that His people were to be outnumbered and a distinct minority in a land and among people more technologically and mechanically advanced than the Israelites. He knew that commercial and contractual dealings with the Canaanites would begin to normalize basic dishonesty. The God of Israel knew that the intermarriage of His people with pagans, especially those as dissolute and immoral as the Canaanites, would lead to swift and thorough perversion and destruction of His institutions of marriage and the family. Above (perhaps below) all God knew that full integration with the Canaanites would lead the Chosen to idolatry, paganism and heathenism and their destruction as a people. Before all this transpired, though, Moses and the Israelites had many miles yet to travel.

Return to the Road

God had instructed Moses to bring the Israelites to Mount Sinai where they would worship Him and receive the Law. The latter they did of a certainty but in the "worship" aspect lay the problems. All serious and sincere Israelites certainly hoped that the quashed rebellion and its motivating spirit were in the past, and looked forward to an open road leading to that land flowing with milk and honey, the Promised Land of Canaan. Most assuredly their leader Moses was eager to get back on the road again.

Perhaps the restart of the journey did not crackle with the electric anticipation of the Exodus from Egypt, but nonetheless the excitement and anticipation factors must have been noticeable. At God's direction Moses had fashioned two beautiful silver trumpets, their blasts and fanfares employed to lead the people. The Israelites were truly blessed and fortunate that, among so many other Divine attributes, their God was an expert in logistics. As before, and just as unappreciated as the blessings were before Sinai, remarkably they were just as scorned after Sinai.

Again, Moses and his flock of Israelites were to be guided over unknown territory by a cloud during the day and a pillar of fire at night, both proving to be more effective than any modern GPS. For provisions, plentiful water, manna, as before, would be provided. Besides, now they were to press forward with a destination awaiting, and it was not a destination far in the distance, Canaan. Obedience and faith, under the guidance of Moses and the auspices of God would guide the Israelites to Canaan. Only two people stood in the way of their promised and anticipated success, the Canaanites and ... the Israelites.

With the exquisitely beautiful deftness of the King James Bible the scriptures record the Israelite resumption of the journey:

> "And it came to pass on the twentieth day of the second month, in the second year, that the cloud was taken up from the tabernacle of the testimony.
> And the children of Israel took their journeys out of the wilderness of Sinai, and the cloud rested in the wilderness of Paran."

Paran, northeast of Sinai, was a harsh locale, as its adjective "wilderness" certainly suggested. Whether history repeats itself is a grand question best left to others, but human beings most decidedly can be repetitive creatures. Soon, once again the Israelites began to engage in whoring and a false nostalgia for Egypt and their apparently delectable diet of cucumbers, melons and all sorts of pleasant spices. "Nothing at all" was their wail, nothing but manna, which apparently tasted like coriander seed, which itself "tasted like oil." Sufficient provender and nutrition they had, but hardly a delicious delicacy.

The burdens upon the Father and His disappointments were becoming more intense, but the Divine Father was not alone, as in a modern vernacular Moses was about to crack. Moses's complaint about his fellow Israelites is well worthy of full quotation, but such would be too tedious. Our scriptural text records that "... the anger of the Lord was kindled greatly" but this time the Israelites found no great intercessor in their leader Moses for "... Moses also was displeased." His anger, too, had become white hot but the main blast of the fury of its flames was aimed not at his fellow Hebrews but rather at God Himself. Moses, an eloquent but plain-speaking man left no emotion hidden from God as:

> "Moses said unto the Lord,
> Wherefore hast thou afflicted they servant; and wherefore have I not found favor in thy sight, that thou layest the burden of all this people upon me."

Even the best, in this case the monumentally great of His servants, Moses, would find cause for anger against God. It is not an uncommon emotion, and is to be noted in both the Old and New Testaments. Just as a child may be angry with a parent at times even the best of disciples (certainly an accurate appellation for Moses) will find moments of frustration and anger with God. The duty and the relief for the disciple is to discern God's reasoning always good and always perfect, in a present dilemma. Moses demonstrated, though, that often when a person feels trapped, treated unfairly and overburdened his real feelings and the more truculent side of his personality will shine through:

> "The people among whom I am, are six hundred thousand footmen, and thou hast said, I will give them flesh that they may eat a whole month. Shall the flocks and the herds be slain for them, to suffice them, or shall all the fish of the sea be gathered together for them to suffice them?"

The sarcasm of Moses's final question to God is unmistakable. As a wise, loving parent, though, God responded to His otherwise exemplary servant not with venom or invective but with generosity. Yet with much of Israel God's patience was a rope which had burned down to the last millimeter. The people are now demanding meat, noticed God, and he assured Moses that He would be generous in providing such. Quails, still prized by many people the world over, but not just a "quail dinner" or quails for a day nor two, nor five, nor ten, nor twenty, but an entire month of the birds. In God's own highly descriptive speech He assured Moses that they would eat quail "... until it came out of your nostrils." Immense flocks of quails arrived and began to fall into the Israelite camp, where many of the recalcitrant Israelites began gorging themselves on the delicacy until a manifestation of God's wrath was visited upon them:

> "And while the flesh was yet between their teeth, ere it was chewed, the wrath of the Lord was kindled against the people, and the Lord smote the people with a very great plague."

Again ingratitude, deep protracted ingratitude had lost the day. For now, though, it was time to put away concerns about diet, taste and nutrition, for the Promised Land of Canaan awaited the dawn of a new era.

CHAPTER SIX

COLLAPSE OF THE ISRAELITES

But not quite yet. Moses, that scripturally ordained "meekest of men" was now to be confronted with the realization of what may be called a dichotomy of problems. Early in our lives we learn that all persons have problems, and no one, neither man nor woman, rich or poor, Jew or Gentile, believer or infidel is exempt. Life, though, seems to be a relentless schoolmaster that teaches us that our problems fall into two broad categories. The first is that ordinary dynamic of difficulty which plagues each and every life, physical maladies, financial difficulties, various fears, mistreatment, even hatred from others and on and on this litany may run. For brevity's sake we shall call them "general" problems, and though common to all humanity they vary with each individual. Then there is that second category of problems, more capable of specific definition and usually more hyper-charged with emotions, more wearing and often more destructive. This is that most bitter category and we shall denominate them as "family problems," with which Moses now came face to face.

Moses had two somewhat famous siblings, his older brother and literal right hand man Aaron, and his older sister Miriam, who had watched for his safety as an infant. Aaron's faith and failures have both been well documented already, but Miriam has remained in a supporting role until now. The scriptures best enunciate and describe this difficulty:

> "And Miriam and Aaron spoke against Moses because of the Ethiopian woman whom he had married for he had married an Ethiopian woman."

The identity of this woman remains unknown and has been a minor point of debate among argumentative scholars. Some have argued that she was Moses's first wife Zipporah (possible but unlikely), but more likely she was a second wife after the Biblically unrecorded death of Zipporah. In any event she was an Ethiopian, which meant that she was black and this an anomaly in a nation of Caucasian Israelites. Perhaps, perhaps even likely, but the true source of resentment of Miriam and Aaron did not lie in racial animus or his marital state but rather in a family emotion which is traced back to Cain and Abel, sibling rivalry and jealousy:

> "And (Aaron and Miriam) said,
> Hath the Lord indeed spoken only by Moses, hath
> he not spoken also by us? And the Lord heard it."

Actually, yes. God was speaking only through Moses. The Lord is the most generous of Fathers in bestowing love, understanding, compassion, grace and every good thing, but He has always been circumspect in assigning authority. The scriptures from beginning to end are an endless demonstration of God's love and patience with His own, usually going far beyond the point(s) at which many good parents will quit. Never, though, has the God of Creation been understanding and patient with those who would challenge His authority.

From the beginning the God of the Universe has been accused by many as being some combination of confusing and ambiguous. To some likely, but to no one, especially Moses, Aaron and Miriam in the events that ensued. God directed the three of them to come to the tabernacle, where they stood in the door of the tent. He called Aaron and Miriam forth, and likely timorous and even shaking they witnessed God come down in a cloud and He made to the pair a special pronouncement:

> "If there be a prophet among you;
> I the Lord will make myself known unto him in
> a vision…
> With (Moses) will I speak mouth to mouth, even
> apparently, and not in dark speeches…"

Emphatically, Moses had been reaffirmed as God's anointed, but the pair of his siblings did not escape the Divine Wrath. Miriam (but not Aaron) was struck with the dread disease of leprosy as her skin became as white as snow. Aaron was in emotional agony over his sister's punishment and begged of Moses that the penalty to Miriam be abated. Moses, in his customary intercessory role, joined his brother in begging God to relent, which He did, but only in part. Miriam, without leprosy, was exiled outside the camp for seven days. When she returned from the brief exile the entire nation resumed the journey and finally reached the wilderness of Paran.

Spies, Reconnaissance and Espionage

When the earliest European colonists to the New World crossed the Atlantic Ocean in the 1600's and landed on the eastern shores of the North American continent it was said that many broke down and wept. No, not really for joy in happiness but for the sudden realization of what lay before them. When they landed on the barren coasts at least in the beginning the land was devoid of habitable dwellings, verdant and fertile farm fields and really any feature whatsoever of civilization. Most tears were shed from shock and fear, dread anticipation of what lay before them as they were charged with making a new home from the wilderness or accept the alternative of death. Not all survived, likely a few decided the New World was not to their liking and returned to England. In the main, though, these hearty but ordinary, even non-descript, men and women, stayed the course and built new lives for themselves, lives of greater freedom, eventually for the many, more prosperity. They faced almost unspeakable hardships, especially at the onset of their odyssey. Almost literally carving new settlements out of an otherwise barren wilderness, enduring severe hot and cold, disease (too often deadly) and understandable resentment from the natives already present, a resentment at times expressed with deadly force, nonetheless they succeeded and established, built and nourished that strip of habitation known as the colonies, which gave birth to the United States of America. Not all were heroes and initially the early settlers were represented by their share of miscreants, malcontents and just bad actors, but these prevailed not. The new settlers, although not wealthy in their native land of England, considered themselves free, and most sought even greater freedom under God. Modern sophisticates may view with haughty disdain their deeds, but good men and true they were. Likely, the modern cynic and hauteur would feel more comfortable with what he would have seen in the camps of the Israelites as they approached the borders of the Promised Land of Canaan.

Among the endless attributes of God as His possession of so many traits that are easily transferred and recognized in human beings. Canaan was a land of strength, in the possession of an especially formidable opponent, the Canaanites, who in so many ways were far more advanced in the complexities of what was then "modern" life. Technologically they were in the vanguard of ancient developments in mobility and weaponry. The people were well organized, independent and not lacking in fighting spirit. The Canaanites had been in the land long enough to erect and develop formidable cities, many of them fortified. Canaan was a "tough nut to crack." The Israelites could not just walk in and take the land, and above all God was so aware.

Among the Almighty's endless list of attributes are many that are unknown and overlooked and central to the present story is that of His generalship. All commanders, excluding the truly incompetent (and they are plentiful in history) know that he needs as much knowledge of the enemy and the presumed battle sites as possible, and God here provides the great example. Before making even an attempt to enter Canaan, God directed Moses, select twelve spies, or perhaps otherwise termed scouts, to enter the land, and conduct a thorough reconnaissance of the territory and its people. The twelve were to represent the Twelve Tribes of Israel, with one man from each tribe to be chosen. Those selected were Shammua, Sophat, Igal, Palti, Gaddiel, Gaddi, Ammuel, Sethur, Nahbi, Gewel, Caleb and Joshua. Except for the final two, they are totally obscure and forgotten in Biblical history. They are worthy of mention, though, because their actions and conduct sit a difficult course of history to Israel for generations to come.

The Israelite spies likely could blend in easily with their Semitic relatives, the Canaanites, and so Moses assigned to them an extensive and intensive plan for scouting. They followed his directions well and went all over the country. They studied the geography and topography of the land and were told to determine whether it was "fat or lean." As fact finders the spies were first rate. They came back after forty days and assured Moses that truly it was a land flowing with milk and honey. It was a rich land abundant with fruits, vegetables, livestock and prosperity. The spies were superior in their location on the peoples who inhabited Canaan, including the Amalekites, the Hittites, the Jebusites and, of course, the Canaanites.

It is now that one of history's greatest examples of two persons (or groups) viewing the same situation and agreeing upon the same facts can arrive at diametrically opposed conclusions. Caleb, in what was apparently a very public report before Moses "...stilled the people before Moses, and said, Let us go up at once, and possess it; for we are well able to overcome it." Joshua, his compatriot, agreed with Caleb. Not so the majority of ten, though, saw a rich land, but not riches only:

> "Nevertheless, the people be strong that dwell in the land, and the cities are walled, and very great; and moreover we saw the children of Anak there."

The overwhelming majority of ten stated flatly that "we be not able to go up against the people, for they are stronger than we." They wailed about the physical stature of the inhabitants and bemoaned that their would-be foes, especially the sons of Anak, were "giants" while they, the poor, weak Israelites were "in our own sight as grasshoppers."

The clichéd response is to aver that the ten Hebrew spies report was a thunderclap of surprise and disappointment to the mass of the Israelites, a teeming mass of some 600,000. A thunderclap is a noisy but brief phenomenon. To the Israelites this report was a raging storm, a tsunami, an earthquake, a massive tornado, a hurricane and whatever other image of destruction may be worked into this picture. All this time, this distance, this uprooting from a settled life in Egypt, an unsavory diet and "problems" galore, only to find that going the last step into the Promised Land was not going to be a walkover and would require spirit, work and prolonged national effort was all too much for the people to bear:

> "And all the congregation lifted up their voice, and cried:and the people wept that night."
> And surprise of surprises (this phrase is sardonic):
> "And all the children of Israel murmured against Moses and against Aaron: and the whole congregation said unto them,
> Would God that we had died in the land of Egypt! or would God we had died in this wilderness?"

Before our narrative resumes its forward thrust let it pause for a moment for some realistic speculation about the Israelites' response to the depressing report of the ten spies. Although this was antiquity still the words of doom spread with supersonic speed throughout the populace. To them Canaan, an admittedly prosperous land, was an Eden if riches with a limitless cache of resources available at the will of the Canaanites. The populace was superhuman in size and capacity, able to flick aside mere mortals of the make of the sons of Israel. Those walled cities between in their thinking and imagery siege proof fortresses impervious to the puny, Lilliputian attacks of the Israelites. It was all so hopeless and foredoomed before it had begun. The dreams of the Promised Land had disappeared as the vapor that appears for a time and then vanishes away. Actually, all of this, at least the now hopeless condition of these people, was true. They had surrendered without the proverbial "shot" being fired. So defeated were the Israelites that they surrendered not to the prospective enemy but to the previous defeated foe, as they wailed:

> "And wherefore hath the Lord brought us unto this land, to fall by the sword, that our wives and our children should be a prey? were it not better for us to return unto Egypt?"

Return to Egypt? This was a land which witnessed their national exodus several years earlier. To return to Egypt, a logistical impossibility without God, would not only be ludicrous but would merit consideration as the most humiliating shame of any nation in all history had ever inflicted upon itself. No, the only path remaining open to the Israelites was the road into Canaan, but...

God's Patience is Exhausted

A good parent is a patient parent (and since for the moment we are speaking of the father we will refer to the parent in the masculine form). He will abide laziness, recalcitrance, whining, ingratitude all the live long day, and then day after day and not explode in anger and retribution upon his own child. He does not delight in severity, harshness and punishment, and the father with the good heart delights in expressing approval and saying "yes" to his children. The bad son or daughter, though, will push the parent to the breaking point to where the parameters of the relationship are changed. God was confronted with an entire nation of bad children, and His patience and forbearance were gone. The punishment for Israel's faithlessness was to be both harsh and historic. He spoke to Moses and Aaron of His anger because of the Israelites' continual murmuring (read "griping") against Him, and His plans for Israel were plainly enunciated:

> "As truly as I live, saith the Lord, as ye have spoken in mine ears, so will I do to you.
> Your carcasses shall fall in the wilderness; and all that were numbered of you, according to your whole number, from twenty years old and upward which have murmured against Me."

Thus the veritable "torch was passed" from not one but all generations save one to the younger generation and those yet unborn. As for the length of their sentence the Israelites were to wander in the famed wilderness for forty years "... until your carcasses be wasted in the wilderness." Only those presently young, the children and the generations to come would see the Promised Land, and the main portion of the Israelites, the people for whom God had performed so many signs and wonders would perish and rot in the desert. God, though, is ever merciful, especially to His faithful and obedient, and we now recall that two of the twelve spies were ready, willing and able to take Canaan. Caleb and Joshua, the latter a man whose name will prove literally to live, forever were spared from the Divine Edict.

Now as for the remainder of the fully "mature" (in years only) nation of Israel a brief resumé of their conduct is in order. After being miraculously freed from the harsh clutches of four centuries of Egyptian slavery they had marched forth in a mass exodus from the power center of Egypt and were led by Moses, likely the greatest single leader in human history. At every sign of trouble or even possible trouble they were more than ready to jettison this entire concept of a Promised Land and return to the relatively safe, but degraded life of the slave. God's answer to their obstinacy was their salvation by the single most spectacular miracle in pre-Christian history, the parting of the Red Sea. Despite their incessant complaining they were catered with food and water in desert lands and with consistency and plenty. Still, they complained, not once, but repeatedly, of the cuisine. At the foot of the Holy mountain of Sinai while Moses was receiving the Law a large number sank to hedonism, heathenism and the basest debauchery. Still, the patience and promises of God held firm, and the Israelites continued forward to the borders of the Promised Land.

Work? Fight? We are expected to take an active part in securing God's promises and our salvation was the outcry. It was too much for the Israelites to bear, and now it had become too much for the Lord of Hosts to bear. They expected everything to be handed to them. The Israelites traditionally had lived the harsh life of slavery, cruel, abject bondage in which they possessed no rights. Yet, slavery itself has certain perimeters and boundaries. As long as they produced for their Egyptian masters their lives and labor were valuable, and would be vouchsafed by their taskmasters. Generation upon cruel generation had taught the Israelites, a people of vast inherent talent and ability, to obey. They were as well-trained farm animals who could and would work but in the midst of generations of servitude has lost all spark and drive. They needed and wanted to be "taken care of," like the citizens (or more appropriately the subjects) of many modern welfare state. Certainly none of these factors absolve the Israelites from blame for their own rebellion, but they provide a partial explanation of what continually being "taken care of" can do to the human spirit.

Hopefully, the previous summary mention of the early American colonists may provide a brief example of a lesson of contrasts. When they came to the untamed wilderness they came as free men and women, not paroled slaves, were accustomed to strain and the hardships of life and labor. They prevailed because to do otherwise was to die. This generation of Israelites failed and were literally left by God to die.

As for this extant failed generation of Israelites their reception of God's judgment of wilderness exile and death was far from joyous. It is fact and not the author's narrative alone which now stretches the image of "childish" Israel still further. As they heard of their fate for the remainder of their lives the people of Israel mourned greatly. Like the child who pushed his parents longsuffering patience past the breaking point Israel, probably through some combination of fear, childish self-assurance and misplaced understanding of the parent Israel finally says, "All right, you win, we will do as you want." So,

> "They rose up early in the morning, and got them
> up into the top of the mountain, saying,
> Lo, we be here, and will go up into the place which
> the Lord hath promised: for we have sinned."

The patience of God, infinitely greater than the patience of man, still has a terminus, that point beyond which even His children cannot go without destruction. Israel had passed that point, and God recognized that dichotomy of "repentance" which is ever present in life. He knew that the Israelites were not really sorry, but rather sorry that they had been caught. Through Moses, He told them simply "don't do it," for your unsanctioned sojourn into Canaan "shall not prosper." God will not be with you, Moses added, and your enemies will win easy victories.

To expect Israel's obedience to God at this juncture would be laughably naïve, and so it was. How man or how large a force entered Canaan is unknown, but the venture was met with disaster. The results of their venture are summarized in a single verse:

> "Then the Amalekites came down, and the Canaanites which dwell in that hill, and smote them, and discomfited them unto Hormah."

God denied them success as years of a rebellious spirit towards Him began to exact their payment from the Israelites. God provided a sterling but stark lesson that while He is always interested and engaged in the affairs of humanity His own people will be decidedly defeated in folly and rebellion. Driven beyond even Divine endurance God here demonstrated that certainly can literally become irredeemable, not by their birth or any other superficial tract but by the hardness of their hearts.

The moral and historical lessons from the forbidden and disastrous Israelite entry into Canaan are a multitude and actually easy to draw. As both Testaments state and, in fact are so underwritten, any venture in direct contravention to God's will is doomed. Sometimes it takes time to so ascertain, but not here, for the Israelites suffered immediate failure. In the harshest and starkest of terms, which modern ears are loath to hear, those that went against the direct commandments of God were destined for death and it would be left to their children only to receive the Divine inheritance. Nowhere in the Old Testament is the basic character and personality of the Creator better told and illustrated than in the story of the Exodus from Egypt and the later collapse of this generation of Israelites (though not of the nation itself). The patience of God, which can really be defined as the continual demonstration of His love, is beyond mortal comprehension, but when it breaks, the thundering reverberations of the break are devastating. All the adults who had rescued from Egyptian bondage, who had thrilled at the miracles of God, who had been fed and watered and whose recalcitrant spirit God had abided for years would now spend the remainder of their days in a pointless (to them at least) wilderness wandering. The basics and necessities of life would be provided, but in modern language they would be enduring life sentences without the possibility of parole. They would literally drop dead and rot in the wilderness.

An interesting but ancient story to be sure but what relevance does it possess for the modern reader or student, even those of a willing heart and a religious bent towards God? The deeply poignant sadness of the story is that it serves as a real metaphor for the story of the majority of the human race, most eloquently stated by Solomon in the Psalms:

> "Except the Lord build the house they labor in
> vain that build it."

Actually the Israelites had built no house, with or without the Lord. For years, even decades, for some they continued to life, to eat, drink, love, and likely find occasional pleasures in the day but to what end? They were all wandering aimlessly, and their paths led to the same earthly terminus, the grave. Just as the Israelites freed from the chains of Egypt chose a path that led to oblivion so also have most of the world's inhabitants to the present. This is not expressed in a spirit of triumph, vindictiveness and hopefully not pride but rather one of stark reality. It is the nature and propensity of humanity to veer life into a direction lacking in meaning and a satisfying direction. Today, every nation is teeming with those living in a wilderness, sometimes a bright, pretty, pleasurable wilderness but often one of sheer drudgery, depression and grayness. Without God, life has no purpose, but with God its purpose is brighter than men and women can even comprehend. One of literature's more famous pessimists and cynics once expressed that "... most men lead lives of quiet desperation." Perhaps, but perhaps not. What most lead and never more perfectly personified than by that generation of Israelites which made the exodus from Egypt are lives lacking in direction and purpose beyond merely reacting to each new day's events and stimuli. Never did a nation more emblemize the yet famous statement from the man putatively the wisest in the world, King Solomon, who stated:

> "Vanity of vanities, saith the Preacher; vanity of vanities, all is vanity."

So it was for the generation of Israel which left Egypt, but Israel's story was not yet fully told.

CHAPTER SEVEN

THE BANNERS OF REBELLION

Even for those without hope life proceeds apace. Forty years would fall, but Israel's younger generation wander without present hope in the wilderness of Paran. These multitudes of Israelites still today provide an almost unparalleled example of both the patience of God and of its breaking. Like all men and women at all times they would wake with the dawning of morning, tend to themselves, their families possessions and responsibilities and sustain themselves with the sustenance given by God. Each and all developed their own routines of life and its seemingly endless pageantry of days, and they interacted with their spouses, children, friends and acquaintances. They had life, shelter, food and water, human companionship and a God who still tended to their daily physical necessities. They were safe from all but the passage and the ravages of death which ends with the terminus and transition for every sentient being. Compared to most people then and now the Israelites were spared so many of life's worries. But their days were long and without substance and direction. The whole nation was bound by barriers, immutable barriers set by the Creator Himself. In this world they lived and died without hope. Each and every aspect of the lives of the Israelites is perfectly matched and synchronized with the life of a man or woman serving life without parole in a maximum-security prison. Yes, it was life, but to what purpose and what end? It remained for one far greater than even Moses a millennium after to remark that "man does not live by bread alone." Like "lifers" in a modern prison they possessed the necessities of life, and just as prisoners do not earn their bed and board neither did the Israelites. To them it was all provided by God.

Our own human reflexes, the Biblical story of the Israelites and our hopefully non-existent but cognizant understanding of life in prison, compels us to further understanding. The Israelites remained unhappy, discontented, bored, restless and most assuredly ready for rebellion and revolution. Whether ancient Israel in the desert wilderness all the way forward to the greatest or most obscure modern state the world has never experienced a shortage of such revolutionary leaders. Whether free, or imprisoned, neither did Israel. During the wilderness years two figures arose that would rattle but not move the foundations of the nation. Whether they acted cooperatively and in tandem or whether they spaced by both time and distance. Acted they did, though, and their names are Korah and Dathan. These two men were not in their pedigree two itinerants who blew across the desert as temporary refuse, and neither were they the sweepings of the street, from which so many modern rebels seem to originate. They were men of pedigree and a distinguished lineage, of special importance to the ancient Israelites. Neither were they solitary rebels, but instead were well supported by men of position and standing. Initially, their planned upheaval contained promise, as it was not without numbers, men of influence and of a general determination to receive what they felt had been rightfully denied them. Their scriptural introduction and partial resumé is so impressive that it merits quotation:

> "Now Korah, the son of Izhar, the son of Kohath, the son of Levi, and Dathan and Abiram, the sons of Eliab, and On, the son of Pelath, sons of Reuben, took men."

While they carried their ancestral glories with them, likewise, did they accumulate the more tangible, as "they rose up before Moses with two hundred and fifty princes of the assembly, famous in the congregation, men of renown." Our narrative should accommodate a brief expository comment about the nature and similarity of revolutions and rebels. Their numbers are too great and their fame or infamy too noteworthy for a listing of historically noteworthy rebels, but almost all have certain things in common. They are usually neither instigated nor financed by lone individuals, but these "rebels" almost always require the backing of large and in one manner or another groups of prestigious persons. The true rebel, the effective revolutionary stands apart and works alone or in the company of a very small group. The "true rebel" focuses his fire not upon people, institutions or nations but upon falsehood. The revolutionary (so many today that they appear to be the majority) seeks fame, adulation and above all power. Dathan, Korah and company, though they may be styled "rebels" were common garden variety revolutionaries. So in that spirit they arose, and so in that spirit we will see them depart the drama.

So, what were the complaints of Korah and cohorts. They were certainly not reluctant to voice their discontent, and especially not even to Moses himself:

> "(T)hey gathered themselves together against Moses and against Aaron, and said unto them, You take too much upon you, seeing all the congregation are holy, every and the Lord is among them – wherefore then lift ye up yourselves above the congregation of the Lord?"

So, they "gathered themselves together," for any collective or mob actions. These were men of mighty self-importance, holding the coveted position and even more coveted title of priest among the Israelite people. Their self-flattering and self-aggrandizement is immediately noticeable as Korah proclaimed that all this congregation "... are holy, every one of them, and the Lord is among them." Korah, with a self-confidence borne and nurtured by the great number of "very important people" at his back than boldly ventured the question to Moses "... wherefore then lift ye up yourselves above the congregation of the Lord?" Korah had that smugness and confidence in his own self-righteousness, the practice of which has never subsided and will never disappear from this world. He has accused Moses and to a lesser degree Aaron of the sin which he is in the midst of committing, that of falsely and with no color of authority from God, that of falsely and with base motives assuming power. Moses had been Divinely selected as God's agent of power, for Moses rightly knew that all real authority lay with God. Yes, Korah wanted power, a highly dangerous and combustible commodity, but not one that is sinful per se. The entirety of the characters and histories of Dathan and Korah are not Biblically revealed, but we are on solid ground when we state that Korah's greatest sin and its source was not power per se, nor fame and notoriety but instead the motivational force behind it, the sin of jealousy or covetousness. Korah wanted what Moses possessed, and he wanted for himself what he saw in Moses. This is a tale whose telling, legends, twists and permutations are legion, and it shall never cease in this life. It is a sin that is haughty, deceitful, very destructive and often killing of both mind and body. Jealousy with Korah was the operative drive, the impelling force, that compelled them forward to attempt to wrest from the hand of Moses the power and authority which had been placed in Moses' hands by God Himself.

Let us, however weakly, but with meekness attempt to define "jealousy." It was one of the Seven Deadly Sins defined by the great Medieval theologian, St. Thomas Aquinas. As usual it was William Shakespeare who centuries later gave it a terminology of literal colorfulness, one common yet today, when he referenced jealousy as the "green eyed monster" in his great tragedy "Othello." Jealousy, or envy if it is preferred, is one of the most inherently dangerous and destructive emotions. Like almost all emotions it is neither intrinsically nor inherently wrong. It was the Creator Himself who proclaimed that He was a "jealous" God. Although invented and exaggerated, worry and fears are often wrong. Husbands and wives are rightfully jealous of the affections and fidelities of their spouses. It is the envy that morphs into covetousness that is so dangerous and displeasing to God. This is the jealousy which Koran, Dathan and cohorts possessed in abundance.

Improper jealousy is an emotion which inherently concedes the moral high ground to the object of the envy. The person who rests in possession of the coveted power, here the fame, recognition and honor which they presumed Moses possessed, has something the other desperately desires. Without delving into morasses of psychology and psychobabble it may be conceded that Korah wished to "be" Moses, the man who he envied above all. For Korah to succeed Moses had to be destroyed or at a minimum, diminished. Such thinking is at the heart of the grasping for political and material power, a grasping which shall never abate. Like so many political candidates, though, Korah offered no reason, no rationale, for his advancement and the "cancelling" of Moses other than himself and his personal desires.

Improper jealousy (and most is) has a viral quality to it. The scriptures list but four specific names, Korah, Dathan, Abiram, and On, but the rebellion spread to some two hundred fifty priests. Like all jealousy it was predicated upon a single inquisitive foundation of "why?" Answering Korah is very simple. It was Moses, not Korah, because God had made the specific choice of Moses to be His agent. Moses had authority, power, responsibility, and fame, and not a single phrase or word in the Bible hints that he ever wanted any of it. From the beginning on Mount Sinai he was a reservoir of reasons and excuses for why he was not suited for the job of deliverer of the Hebrews. This longtime shepherd was the Divinely affirmed "meekest of men" and himself was a man who continually spoke to God to dissuade Him from punishing or even destroying the Israelites. So maybe Korah was right in that Moses took upon himself too much; if he meant too much work, too much responsibility, too much worry and too many problems. So let it be as it may, said God, and He gave to Moses instructions to convey to Korah, directions to Korah that would allow the matter of authority to be settled with some finality.

Before the narrative of Korah proceeds to its denouement let it be temporarily diverted to the historically ruinous effects of jealousy, a sin of which in any manner Korah invented. Let our telling be in reverse as the most recent scriptural drama concerning envy was played out only shortly before the rise of Korah, in the persons of Moses's own siblings, Aaron and Miriam (see Chapter Six). The entire Israelite nation effectively had long been jealous of its own self, continuing whining and bemoaning the remembered comforts and luxuries of its past as the slaves of the Egyptians. The Israelite nation itself had landed in Egypt largely due to the fraternal jealousies and hatreds which had arisen, festered and poisoned the brotherly relationships between Joseph and ten of his brothers. That family of men had exceedingly apt teachers in their father and uncle, Jacob and Esau, a swindler and a bon vivant, the latter a would-be murderer of the former. The parents of Jacob and Esau had given a mighty theatrical effect to envy as mother Rebekah costumed her son Jacob to cheat her other offspring, Esau, of his birthright. Backward on backward runs the historical clock, and we see Lot jealous of the prosperity of his uncle Abraham. Then the early pages of Genesis reveal the natural ends of extreme jealousy when Cain cold-bloodedly murders a much better man, his younger brother Abel. Neither does jealousy end with Korah, for the remainder of the Biblical story throughout the Old and New Testaments is filled with the evil of jealousy and its horrid effects. It is, though, appropriate to focus the mind's gaze upon the earthly birth of jealousy, a birth and its offspring, which is still being honed to desire perfection by its midwife, Satan.

The earthly beginning (the War in Heaven is beyond our ken) commences in Eden itself, that Garden of Perfection and perhaps at least a partial preview of Heaven itself. Men and women and the magnificent and beloved animal kingdom living in perfect harmony and in a perfect beautiful environment, endless, ever giving. All was done under the presence, the love and the auspices of the Father and Creator, God Himself. One, only one guideline, or prohibition, the partaking of the fruit of the heir of the Knowledge of Good and Evil was forbidden. It was paradise, perfection, Heaven itself, until the entry of one being and one suggestion. The Devil, in the entry of one being and one suggestion. The Devil, in the form of a serpent (read snake) entered the premises and made a suggestive temptation which he hoped and did partially succeed for a time in turning and changing the course of the universe. Eat of the tree, he told Adam and Eve, and your eyes shall be opened to the real truth. Rather than the receipt of death's promise which God Himself had assured, you shall receive wisdom, knowledge and all its benefits and "... yet shall be as gods." Satan dug a deep well, a chasm in fact, from which lessons are to be drawn, but central in his assurance to humanity that "you do not need God, for you yourselves can be gods." If a person can be a god himself, why does he need the one true god? This remains not just the heart, but the soul and substance of much sin, from the first man and woman to the twenty-first century. Why do I need God and why do I need his system and restraints when I can be a deity myself? This is the highest (or perhaps the better nomenclature is the "lowest") of all jealousy.

Korah, Dothan, and their followers proposed, likely without any prior or deep philosophical or theological examination, to substitute their judgment for God's. they "knew better." God was with Moses, sympathized with him and most certainly supported his great prophet, but He knew that at its base Korah's attack was an attempted blow to His own authority. God now determined that it was time that He settled with this latest upstart.

The "showdown" would be tomorrow. Among other things God has always been a great dramatist and occasionally has been known to arrange an appointed place and time for a demonstration of Divine Power. It fell to Moses to advise Korah of the particulars and specifications:

> "Moses spoke unto Korah and unto all his company, saying,
> Even tomorrow the Lord will show who are His, and who is holy; and will cause him to come near to Him whom He hath chosen will He cause to come near unto Him."

Korah and his company (perhaps mob would be a better term) were to take censers, vessels used to burn incense light them afire and present them to God the next day Moses could not restrain himself from making biting remarks to Korah indicating his disdain for these men who wanted more than they were assigned, but in any event the matter would be settled after the rising of the next day's sun.

Of Korah we have built the story around him, but what now of the aforementioned Dathan and Abiram? They proved to be even more recalcitrant than Korah and told Moses simply "We will not come up." They halted not, though, with a simple refusal, even a sarcastic "no, thanks" but instead answered Moses with a bill of indictment which began:

> "Is it a small thing that thou hast brought us up out of a land that floweth with milk and honey, to kill us in the wilderness, except thou make thyself altogether a prince over us?"

So, enough time and events had elapsed that Egypt, the actual land of cruel slavery, had assumed in their minds that golden chimera of a land "flow(ing) with milk and honey." It is not an absurdity that in the exodus, on that day of release and freedom, both Dathan and Aberian well among the multitudes with broad smiles on their faces. Now, though, the remembrances had evolved into other images entirely. The refusal of compliance ended with a bitter pirouette of venom:

> "Moreover thou hast not brought us into a land that floweth with milk and honey or given us inheritance of fields and vineyards: will thou put out the eyes of these men?
> We will not come up."

So was the story of Dathan and Aberian.... for the moment.

Moses was as human as any individual who ever drew breath, and by this stage of life he had accumulated worlds of accusations regarding his supposed evil, his perfidy and self-aggrandizement, all in a position he neither sought nor ever wanted. He defended himself with the lament that he had never personally profited from his position of leadership, had never so much as taken "one ass from them," and in general his soul was bone-weary of such accusations. For the present, though, the Lord turned His Divine attention to just that, the present. He began to set a scene, extensively dramatic in itself, but definitely suggestive of an even more spectacular moment which would occur a few centuries at a place called Mount Carmel. A test of strength, power and authority, most decidedly public, was in the offing.

The contest, the setting, and contestants was directed by God through Moses. On one side every man, including Korah and his two hundred fifty adherents was to bring his censer, and each was to place incense in their vessel. On the other side were Moses and Aaron, the chief priest, and he was to do likewise. As was done in the customary tabernacle worship they were to place fire into each censer, but now Korah and company were totally segregated from Aaron and Moses. The latter pairs order for separation was accompanied with God's frightfully ominous words of "separate yourselves from this congregation, so that I may consume them in a moment." Certainly Korah, but neither were Dathan and Aberian forgotten by God. All the Israelites who had assembled were told to "depart from the tents of those wicked men" and so they "... got up from the tabernacle of Korah, Dathan and Aberian, the miscreants themselves along with their families appearing and standing in the doors of their tents.

With the stage set and the players in their places it befell Moses to speak, and as he almost always responded he spoke for God. The decision is the Lord's, Moses announced, whether these men who had led a revolution would die or "would suffer the common death of all men." Rarely have starker and more harshly foreboding words been uttered than what Moses now announced:

> "If the Lord make a new thing, and the earth open her mouth and swallow them up, with all that appertain to them, and they go down quick into the pit: then you shall understand that those men have provoked the Lord."

The Lord of Hosts, the loving Creator, that most patient of beings is a longtime losing it. He abides beyond what not even the best of His Creation, the finest men and women, will tolerate, save for one matter. He never absorbed and abided rebellion and a direct challenge to His authority, and Korah's rebellion would be no exception. "Provoked the Lord" at this juncture is a mild phraseology, inasmuch as the seemingly inexhaustible patience of God had been taken for granted but in actuality was being drained from a Divine reservoir the moment the Israelites left Egypt. For Korah and his accomplices to still be so self-serving and self-exulting at this date was more than God could bear:

> "And it came to pass as (Moses) had made an end of speaking all these words that the ground clave asunder and was under them.
> And the earth opened up her mouth and swallowed them up, and their houses, and all the men that appertained unto Korah and all their goods."

(only the King James version of the Old Testament could issue a phrase so eloquent and hauntingly descriptive as "the earth opened her mouth") to describe mass death. But even now God was not placated for after Korah and the other leaders were swallowed up:

> "There came out a fire from the Lord, and consumed the two hundred and fifty men that offered incense."

At least for the moment the punishments of God meted out by the words of Moses had their effect, for "... all Israel that were round about them fled at the cry of them for they said Lest the earth swallow us up also."

Among His endlessly inexhaustible Divine attributes is God's propensity to utilize every situation, each event, all thoughts, for a plethora of lessons. God demonstrated His adamancy that He was the determinant of the order not of His Universe, His Creation but also of His relationship to His disciple, the Israelites. Not only Korah, Dathan and Abiram had attempted to overthrow Gpd's plans but so also did the two hundred fifty false priests, their remains now nestled within the bosom of the earth. The "brazen censers" which the false priests had fashioned were taken, offered to God and then placed as "broad plates" for a covering of the altar. Eleazar, Aaron's son, and a legitimate priest, oversaw this operation.

As for the priesthood itself God reiterated His original conception and plan and said this is the new alter, that it was to be:

> "(A) memorial unto the children of Israel, that
> no stranger which is not of the seed of Aaron,
> came near to offer incense before the Lord; that
> to be not as Korah, and as his company: as the
> Lord said to him by the hand of Moses."

But the souls of tranquility and serenity lay not within the Israelite people. Without breaking stride the very next day it is to be found not a renewed commitment to God but the old, sad story of the Israelite slaves who had been redeemed from Egyptian bondage:

"But on the morrow all the congregation of the children of Israel murmured against Moses

and against Aaron saying, You have killed the peoples of the Lord."

He had reached His Divine limits and breaking point. After their liberation from Pharaoh, the Divine catering of food and water, continual rebellion, both actual and threatened God, like the endlessly patient good parent was ready to unleash His wrath as He now directed Moses to:

> "Get you up from among this congregation, that
> I may consume them as in a moment.
> And they fell upon their faces."

Moses, ever obedient to God but also ever solicitous of his people, the Israelites (thus a man who was both the ideal leader and the ideal servant), told Aaron to quickly enter the tabernacle and make an atonement for the people. The atonement was made by placing fire from the altar upon the incense, which Aaron did with dispatch and "stood between the dead and the living." A total of 14,700 Israelites died from a plague sent by God, but the effects of which were stayed by the atoning offering of Moses and Aaron. The plague was finished, but the sickness in the spirit of Israel remained.

Israel in the wilderness was a discontented and unhappy nation, and God seemed not to care. More accurately expressed "God did not care." They had become the Bible's foremost example of a people to whom the love and mercies of God were granted abundantly, always without a reciprocal gratitude, much less love for the Heavenly Father. The God of Israel was literally waiting for the older generation to gradually die off in the wilderness, and such was happening year by year. In the meantime other than God, one great constant remained still. That was Moses, but for how much longer?

CHAPTER EIGHT

FROM MOSES TO JOSHUA

Forty years is a large proportion of the lifespan of any person, including many historical and Biblical noteworthiness who never even came close to celebrating a fortieth birthday. Military leaders and world conquerors such as Alexander the Great, famous men of the fine arts such as Raphael the painter, the composers Mozart and Schubert, the famous trio of early nineteenth century English Romantic poets, Byron, Keats and Shelley ad infinitum never saw forty and some in this list never even experienced a thirtieth year of life yet God had condemned all those Israelites passing twenty years of age to wander on the wilderness for forty years in punishment for the hardened recalcitrance of their spirit. Naturally the curious inquiry is one of what happened during these four decades.

Without any sense of humor or irony we assert that naturally "death" happened, as it was so intended. The family of the leader and most prominent Israelite, Moses, was not exempt from the curse. The first and beloved wife of Moses, Zipporah, a Midianite woman who had died sometime earlier was the first to pass, which event trained an unaccustomed spotlight upon the conduct and attitude of Miriam. While not a figure of towering importance her life holds great significance and is worthy of notice and examination. Miriam appears first long before in the days of Egyptian slavery as the older sister but likely still a young girl herself who tends the infant Moses until he is rescued (from the Nile River) by Pharaoh's daughter. She is then the liaison between the great Egyptian lady and her own mother, Jochebed, and thus a major foundational stone in the early life of Moses.

The Exodus not primarily a story of Moses's family, but she next appeared unfortunately as a complainer and murmurer against the widower Moses's second wife, a Cushite woman. For her complaining spirit and incipient rebellion she was exiled outside the Hebrew camp for seven days (see Chapter 5). Miriam was a woman of such stature that she was denominated a prophetess, and was likely a figure of consistent significance in the Israelite camp. Finally, she succumbed to death in the fortieth and final year of Israel's wanderings. She would have been a very aged lady, and her death is noted without elaboration or apparent memorializing but simply that it was in the first month of the fortieth year and that "Miriam died in (Kadesh) and was buried there."

But what of the nation itself for these forty years? Of all the history of Israel from the Exodus forward this is a period of perhaps the greatest sparsity of scriptural description of the nation, although still we are not lacking in information. What we know is entirely, if disappointingly and unpleasantly, consistent with Israel's prior history. The one recorded event of national significance during the forty years is one of the Bible's most macabre and ghoulish stories, a tale of reptilian horror.

The Plague of the Snakes

The forty-year period of wandering was rapidly expiring, and geographically the Israelites, now a people bolstered for almost two generations of wilderness hardening was at the brink of entering the Promised Land. Their leaders remained the same as forty years before, Aaron, the high priest and the progenitor of the priesthood that would forever bear his name and Moses, the Lord's appointed Deliverer himself, who yet remained strong in his position. Each was soon to receive sad, even shocking news, and the first blow landed on Aaron when God called the two brothers together atop Mount Hor to hear God's direction:

> "Aaron shall be gathered unto his people: for he shall not enter into the land which I have given unto the children of Israel, because you rebelled against My word at the water of Meribah."

Meribah's story, which was equally vital to the future of Moses will be discussed somewhat later, but for now suffice it to say that the rebellion of God's direct command there by Aaron was the impetus for God's decision that Aaron's time of departure was near. Aaron's son, Eleazar, his designated successor as high priest was given the priestly robes and regalia of his father, while Aaron, Eleazar and Moses returned to Mount Hor, where Aaron died.

Aaron was a major figure in the history of Israel, though certainly not the equal of his younger brother Moses, who overshadowed him in importance, courage and character. Sadly, Aaron's most memorable moment was at the foot of Mount Sinai, where he succumbed to the mob and their likely threats to fashion a manufactured idol. In this world his name and legacy will always be tarnished by the execrable behavior, but

Aaron remained a man of substance for decades. Faithfully he served as high priest for decades, and while working under the supervision and the shadow of Moses, Aaron was at his best. Flawed though he was, as are all, Aaron was a faithful man and served well both Israel and God.

Still, the Deliverer, the presumably indispensable man, Moses, remained among the living, his strength, health, faculty and abilities amazingly undiminished. Such was good, too, because after generations God was preparing to lead the Israelites into the Promised Land. Undoubtedly, the Israelite population sensed, if they knew not the specifics, that the day of their entry into Canaan was at hand. As all people at all times they spoke of it to each other, with excitement, wonder, relief, trepidation and outright fear of what was now not a distant chimera but a very likely, promising, but yet ominous event in the immediate offing. They spoke of other things as well, and to demonstrated that still they were well placed in that long continuum of Hebrew generations they were "murmuring."

Under the leadership of Moses the Israelites, now on the very cusp of the land flowing with milk and honey, fought their first battle against the Canaanites and war. In the stark militarily historical descriptions of the Book of Numbers "... the Lord hearkened to the voice of Israel, and delivered up the Canaanites, and they utterly destroyed them and their cities, and He called the name of the place Hormah." Egypt, slavery, the parting of the Red Sea and other historically seminal events were daily receding into the past to be "history" and national lore, but certain constants remained part and parcel of the Israelite nation. At the top of the list is an old familiar complaint best expressed by the Israelites themselves:

> "And the people spoke against God and against Moses.
> Wherefore have you brought us up out of Egypt to die in the wilderness? for there is no bread, neither is there any water: and our soul loatheth this light bread (i.e. Manna)."

These are not the voices of the generations that were warped by slavery and the petulant childishness which it engendered, but rather the younger generations that were specifically saved and protected by God for the purposes of establishing His earthly Kingdom in the Promised Land of Canaan. Yet again God hears a disharmonious clanging complaint from His Chosen nation, even in the wake of a great victory He has given them.

Like the parent who has finally been pushed too far God's response to His Israelites is a great leap forward in discipline and punishment from what has gone before. This time they will suffer no plagues, no fires and neither will the earth open its jaws to swallow the recalcitrant. God's response was simple and simply expressed:

> "And the Lord sent fiery serpents among the people, and they bit the people, and much people of Israel died."

From the Fall in Eden snakes have not merely symbolized but in their slimy, slithering have literally embodied the fears and terrors of all rational persons (including, perhaps with special emphasis, the writer of these words). They are deadly terrors whose very presence and threat represent Satan and evil incarnate. Yet it is not all religions or mystical metaphor, for many are deadly, including these now unleashed upon the Israelites.

To perish by snakebite is more than death itself. It is as Satan himself with all the torments of fear, terror and pain has marked a person for eternal pain. The snakes were sliding their repulsive bodies everywhere, and the people begged for deliverance. To Moses they admitted that:

> "We have sinned, for we have spoken against the
> Lord, and against thee; pray unto the Lord, that
> He take away the serpents from us.
> And Moses prayed for the people."

God's answer to the prayers was Divinely unique, comforting and most of all completely thorough. He was given a command to:

> "Make thee a fiery serpent, and set it upon a pole:
> and it shall come to pass, that every one that is
> bitten, when he looketh upon it he shall live."

Indeed it was a strange cure for a poisonous snake bite but "... if a serpent had bitten any man, when he beheld the serpent of brass." This incident and symbol, though, has been a venerable emblem lasting three- and one-half millennia. Known as a caduceus he maintains a prominence in the twenty-first century and remains a universally recognized symbol of the healing arts and the medical profession.

The Israelites repented and were ready to engage fully in the conquest and settlement of the Promised Land. Now, though, and for the first time in generations the stories of Israel and Moses would separate. Sometime earlier, even as they were nearing the end of the wilderness wanderings in the Desert of Zin the Israelites engaged in their oldest and most favorite refrain that they wished "... that we had died when our brethren died before the Lord." This also occurred at the same juncture where the Israelites again needed water. God instructed Moses to take a rod and with Aaron go to a rock and speak to the rock so that it would give water. Moses, who certainly possessed a temper, followed God's instructions but only to a point. He went to the rock but instead of speaking his anger, overcame his judgment, and twice he struck the rock. Nonetheless, God still provided the water for Israel, but the days of Moses were now numbered. God determined that the great leader would view the Promised Land but would depart this present world before entering Canaan.

A Summation of Moses

Never before nor since has one man been so identified with the birth of a nation, not to mention an entire spiritual dispensation and epoch of history, as is Moses with ancient Israel. Perhaps the only man who comes close is the first American president, George Washington the father of his country, a man of towering capability and character but also one who was ably assisted by other great men, many historical giants themselves. Moses, though, still stands alone, incapable of being diminished by later historians and theologians whose skills are greater than their historical and spiritual judgment.

Just how great was Moses and how important was his character? Perhaps it comes to mind two phrases, coined in modern times, to describe a man of varied and superlative talents. These are "a man for all seasons" and a "Renaissance man", which are capable of shifting meanings yet are of extreme admiration no matter the definition. In the most basic of terms they describe a man whose character is so well developed that he is a worthy opponent for any and all of life's challenges. The fabled

Renaissance man is that person possessing an entire metric of many talents, all and each of which are sturdy and adaptable at a standard to meet all encountered problems. All these superlatives are clearly applicable to Moses, but oddly enough even in the text of the Holy Bible he possessed no special aura that seemed to call the attention to any one quality. He is a man whose life begs for deeper study of the individual coherent parts to find any reasonable answer to the question "why did God chose Moses from among the many?"

The life story of Moses conveniently divides itself into three rather distinct chapters, each, at least from a superficial deliberation, radically different one from another. From the beginning his very existence seemed to be a personal affront to a line of kings who were in the times the most powerful men on earth, the Egyptian Pharaohs. As an infant, a Hebrew baby marked for death, he was rescued from the Nile River by Pharaoh's daughter. From the outset he was extraordinarily well placed in Pharaoh's royal palace with access to the best from the most profoundly developed nation on earth, Egypt, the best education, manners, knowledge of the Egyptian culture, while himself remaining a Hebrew, and doubtless never losing touch with his Hebrew heritage, his own Hebrew mother, Jochebed, playing a vital role.

The middle portion of Moses's life generally is a period of scriptural silence but likely of immense and unrecognized importance in the molding of his life and leadership qualities. He lived a normal life, worked exceptionally hard and had a wife, Zipporah, of high moral quality, and a son. The Moses of Biblical fame, even centrality, his cultural significance, religious importance and unfinished fame was formed in his life in the Egyptian royal house and as a Midianite shepherd. The nature and exactitude of the character of this monumental figure who was called by God in the Burning Bush is worthy of a brief examination.

The life of neither man nor woman has been fashioned for easy separate, even isolated analysis of its parts. Each life is a whole, an animate body, solid working harmoniously within itself but also capable of being analyzed in parts. An element of the character of Moses which undoubtedly was attractive and pleasing to God was his humility, a quality highly prized in Heaven, whatever the time. The first third of his life was passed as a noteworthy and high-ranking Egyptian, but no evidence may be found to show that Moses ever sought to make capital of this fact. He fled the potential wrath of Pharaoh and other authorities to live a pastoral existence for the middle third of his life. Here he was successful, and he seems to have found tranquility and domestic serenity as a successful shepherd and loving husband and father until the Lord called him on that momentously fateful day to the Burning Bush.

Historically and even Biblically so many men are driven to great heights (and sometimes depths) of power, fame and prestige by an insatiable lust for personal glory. When Moses faced God for that first time on Sinai, though, this was a man as far from self-extolling of his own virtues and abilities as a man could be. God gave him a commission to return to the Israelites in Egypt, a people and a land now alien to him, confront the most powerful man in the world, secure the release of upwards of a million souls from slavery, cross a desert and form a new nation With the exception of the mission which was born with a child in an obscure village some fifteen hundred years later this was the most colossal task ever given a human being. Moses himself was awed, and genuinely attempted to deflect God's desire with sincere confessions of his own shortcomings. God demurred, and Moses persisted with one reason and/or excuse after another attempting to deflect the Divine burdens about to fall upon him. The people do not know me he protested, and neither am I a very good speaker. Although God's patience was tested with the endless litany of Moses's self-imprecations his recitation of them was sincere and evidenced a trait that is often impossible to find in powerful leaders, humility. It was a character strength evidenced by Moses for his entire life and places him in an exceedingly favorable light.

Moses was a very self-effacing man, especially for one who was in the fore of all Israel for generations. The Torah discloses no incidents of self-dealing or self-aggrandizing behavior. He was that rare leader who truly saw himself in a dual role, both as a servant of his people and ultimately as a servant of his God. Actually, much of the greatness of Moses as a leader and as a man may be found in the intersection of these two roles of service, to God and to his fellow Israelites. Moses often seemed to be that family member who constantly strains and labors to keep the familial bonds of the family unbroken.

No man nor woman, including Moses, lives a life of compartmentalization of his traits, both virtuous and disadvantageous. To a Christian and to what was once called Christendom likely Moses most admirable, sterling and lasting character attribute is his activity, often of jaw-dropping courage, as an intercessor between God and the Israelites. Here, more than once he acted in a dual role as both an intercessor to calm the fury of the Almighty and to protect his erring family members. When Moses descended Mount Sinai with the Law he was amazed, aghast and infuriated to see that the Israelites had descended into the hell and wretchedness of idolatry. Nothing, though, may have flabbergasted him more than to witness that his trusted brother's courage and faith had been discarded in his fashioning of the golden calf. Moses was angry, disappointed and perhaps somewhat heartbroken to see his older brother descend to such depths. His character, though, was proven golden, and his backbone one of steel, as Moses assuaged the wrath of God, a wrath which He wished to visit upon Aaron. Years later, not only Aaron but also his sister Miriam tested God to the breaking point with their incipient rebellion which was fueled by their jealousy of Moses. Again, Moses stepped between his siblings sin and shame and the justified wrath of God to ameliorate the penalties placed upon his brother and sister.

We remember that not once, but multiple times, God's patience had been stretched and broken when He had a change of the Divine Heart and wished to alter the course of His Divine plans for salvation from the nation of Israel to the lineage of Moses. Moses's skill and character were so developed that He dissuaded God from such, and the Lord adhered to His original plans. Of course, the Torah is resplendent with many other examples of the intercession of this great man and prophet, Moses.

Power and its continual exercise alters the course of the character of a man or woman, but apparently Moses was a shining example. One of history's most famous aphorisms is from the nineteenth century English historian Lord Acton who famously remarked that "... power corrupts, and absolute power corrupts absolutely." Moses, though, provides a beautiful exception, and nary a whiff of "corruption "of character has ever arisen from the story of his life.

It may be trite but also true that in the world all good things come to an end, and the magnificent and exemplary life of Moses was not accorded a cloak of exception. So many years had now passed, and the generation of Egyptian slavery had expired in the wilderness. The Israelites were now in Kadesh, at the border of the Promised Land, and in the spirit of a well-entrenched national tradition they were still complaining, and that of a familiar subject, a dearth of water. God directed Moses to speak to a rock from which the water would miraculously flow. Moses, his temper rather undiminished after all these years, was angry at his fellow countrymen and instead he struck the rock with his shepherd's rod. Although God still provided the water, He exacted a punishment from Israel's great leader:

> "And the Lord spoke unto Moses and Aaron, because you believed Me not, to sanctify Me in the eyes of the children of Israel, therefore you shall not bring this congregation into the land which I have given thee."

Long have even disciples and believers questioned the supposed unreasonable harshness of God in denying Moses entry into Canaan. Yes, Moses, was aging, but this was just one transgression, it may be argued. Of course Moses had aged but unlike so many leaders who overstay their competence and age the Torah is explicit in assuring its readers that even though Moses was aging "... his eye was not dim, nor his natural force abated."

God is not required to justify His ways nor His decisions to His creation, yet may we not engage in a bit of speculation? For over four decades Moses had obeyed God and had masterfully served Him while still being a great shepherd to his flock. Moses's time, though, great as it was, had reached its terminus, and a new leader was a necessity for new, onerously burdensome tasks.

Moses is impossible to summarize in a pithy biographical paragraph. Until the birth of Jesus of Nazareth in the village of Bethlehem he was the most important and significant man who has ever lived. As a leader of Israel he was incomparable, never equaled and given the accolade that Israel never saw another prophet the equal of Moses. Even in the New Testament so prominent did he remain that he is referenced seventy-nine times, appeared in Heavenly form on the Mount of Transfiguration and was continually cited by Christ Himself. Did God have any man who could replace him?

The passing of Moses from this terrestrial world to the next was calm and unspectacular, actually as his lifelong character had proven to be. "Not spectacular?" A knowledgeable student might ask, the life of a man who fled from Egypt as a fugitive, then confronted Pharaoh face-to-face, brought down ten plagues upon Egypt, led a massive horde of people in the most storied immigration in history, received the Divine Law directly from God Himself and then led His chosen people for forty years? The events, moments of drama and chronology of the life of Moses who ever lived. His character, though, was greater than mere spectacle. It was well rooted, deep, steadfast, and always dependable and faithful. In the midst of rebellion and havoc the inner soul and spirit of Moses seemed ever tranquil. Israel was ever at war with God, but Moses was never at war with his own countrymen and certainly not with God. Moses was a man whose soul was ever at peace, and he merited a peaceful passing into the next life.

God had Moses exit this mortal coil with his beloved nation of Israel in as good condition as possible. The impending death of Moses was publicized throughout the nation as well as the identity of his successor. It was Joshua, the man who is about to become the central Israelite protagonist in our story, and a man himself worthy of vast and deep study and consideration. For the moment, though, our gaze remains upon Moses in his exit. Moses and Joshua appeared before a gathering of the elders of Israel, where for the last time Moses delineated certain rites and commandments they were to follow, and formally passed the cloak of leadership to Joshua. It was not an especially tearful, maudlin or sentimental gathering, though, as Moses had been there every step of the way with his stubborn and recalcitrant countrymen, and thus he expressed:

> "For I know that after my death you will utterly corrupt yourselves, and turn aside from the way which I have commanded you, and evil will befall you in the latter days; because you will do evil in the sight of the Lord, to provoke him in anger through the work of your hands."

A not particularly ingratiating or encouraging benediction, but sadly a true one.

God led Moses from the plains of Moab to Mount Nebo, and from there showed Moses much of the Promised Land which he had tirelessly and faithfully led the Israelites. The monumentally great leader died there in the land of Moab and there was buried in a valley. Thirty days of mourning were proclaimed for Israel, and so the people wept and mourned. Scripturally proclaimed as Israel's greatest prophet and leader, it is neither vainglorious nor an exaggeration to opine that Moses yet remains the single greatest leader among all mortal men. Could Joshua replace such a man?

CHAPTER NINE

JOSHUA LEADS THE WAY

The God of Creation has a marvelous aptitude for surprise, often and especially when it comes to His selection of certain men and women for the Divinely ordained work. Abram was a man of no special renown when he was summoned from Ur of the Chaldees to be the progenitor of a great nation, many people from which would come the most important person ever born. The mother of that baby, little Mary, a teenage girl deep in the obscurity of a Galilean village was certainly no great glamorous princess living in a palace. Almost all the Old Testament prophets were men plucked from ordinary lives to perform great tasks. Likely the most surprising of all, though, were the men which Jesus of Nazareth plucked not just from obscurity, but from anonymity to become His apostles, the very foundation of His church which would live forever. Peter, Andrew, James, John, Nathanael and Thomas were "blue collar" fishermen, and Matthew was a dread publican, a tax collector, his only fame was an infamy of ill feeling, venom and outright animosity, even hatred, which many of his countrymen felt for him.

Still, God was not a Divine magician constantly amusing people and history with his choices. At times they were obvious and of undeniable logic. Certainly this was true in the selection of Joshua to be the successor to Moses. He was the son of a man named Nun, and he made an auspicious debut as a young man when Moses selected him for a role of paramount importance in the period after the exodus and the parting of the Red Sea. An early and inveterate enemy of Israel were the Amalekites, who blocked the Israelites' path following their Egyptian departure. The Amalekites, experienced and skilled warriors, were known to be planning an attack upon Israel. Moses selected Joshua to lead the Hebrew nation's soldiers in battle, and thus Joshua began his famed career in a role for which he would achieve lasting fame, his prowess and ability as a military commander, who along with David may be accounted as one of Israel's two greatest on the battlefield. Under the remote and noninterfering leadership of Moses, Joshua led the Israelites to a smashing victory. Already at a youthful but indeterminate age this talented and courageous young man from the tribe of Ephriam had established a substantial personal record.

Unsurprisingly Joshua was chosen as his tribe's representative when Moses dispatched the twelve scouts (historically termed "spies") to reconnoiter the land of Canaan before its invasion. The ten-man majority returned frightened and faithless and in abject gloom and defeat that the Canaanites and their cities were too powerful for Israel to take. Only Joshua and his colleague Caleb dissented and with a steadfast faith assured Moses that the land could be taken. The subsequent events have previously been described at some length, and it remains only for us to reiterate that only Joshua and Caleb among the Israelites over twenty years of age would be permitted entrance into Canaan.

Doubtless Joshua was a man, even when young, who was continually associated with Moses. He, of course, did not ascend Mount Sinai with Moses to receive the Law, but it was Joshua who faithfully kept a vigil awaiting the return of Moses. The scriptures describe Joshua as the "minister" of Moses, and young Joshua awaited his leader's return from the slopes. He waited, and waited and then waited some more, and in this interregnum the idolatry of Israel was given full sport at the base of Sinai. Joshua literally awaited "betwixt two" paths, that of God and idolatry below. He was so concerned that when Moses finally descended Joshua greeted Moses with the exclamation that "… there is a noise of war in the camp," yet Moses knew that it was something even worse as Moses explained that it was not the noise of was but the voice of revelry, song and idolatry. The superstructure of the character of Joshua was now not only revealed but highlighted. In that eternal struggle between right and wrong, good and evil and God and Satan, Joshua would always choose God.

When Moses handed Joshua his staff and placed the mantel of leadership upon Joshua's shoulders, he was passing the responsibility of leadership to a man of great talents, leadership skills tested in the cauldron of conflict and battle and superb moral character. Still, Joshua faced what men and women learn and relearn from generation to generation. The final step from number two to number one may be gargantuan, and quite often aspirants for leadership are tripped up. The vice-president of an organization may be dedicated and talented in his sphere but stumbles when thrust into the presidency. Even more prosaically the step from assistant head coach of a football team to the head coach's position may prove the proverbial bridge too far.

Let us push away from our consideration the triteness of the fact that Joshua was not Moses. Of course he was not, as no person, whatever the roles or the similarity of character and actions is the duplicate of another. Joshua possessed certain advantages which were denied Moses. He had been born and reared in Egypt as a slave and had lived his entire life as an Israelite. Moses came to his people much later in his life, and though he was as much an Israelite as any he had been nurtured in a royal palace and had lived most of his days as a Midianite shepherd. As the scriptural narrative starkly and thoroughly explains Moses and the Israelites had to be introduced one to the other, and their relationship seemed always to be smoldering with unrest and animus at least from the masses of the Hebrews. Joshua was "one of them," known by them, never an Egyptian nor a Midianite and never anything but an Israelite. The people knew him, their elders, priests and leaders knew him, and in the beginning was no lack of good will.

As the Israelites began to draw together and organize for their great incursion into Canaan many of their leaders made an apparent heart-warming promise to Joshua:

> "As we hearkened unto Moses in all things, so
> will behearken unto thee: only the Lord they
> God be with thee, as He was with Moses."

Truly inspiring, encouraging words, yet the sardonic cynic might observe that these beautiful words were more of a threat than a comforting promise. Joshua very well knew that the Israelites' history with Moses primarily had been disobedience, complaint, murmuring and rebellion. Could he expect and would he receive better from his countrymen than did the magnificent Moses?

Espionage – Round Two

It is tempting and easy to reference Israel as a monolithic mass of people acting, thinking and moving as one. Almost one-fourth of the Israelites had already crossed into Canaan and settled on the east side of the Jordan River, the forever famous stream that traversed much of the land from north to south. These were the tribes of Reuben, Gad and half the tribe of Manasseh who had already settled there. Joshua, though, needed his entire military strength for the conquest of Canaan. Further, perhaps even more cogently he wanted a united Israel and for all to take part in the conquest of Canaan. He allowed them to remain settled and their women and children to remain protected. He issued his command, though, that "...you shall pass before your brethren arrived, all the mighty men of valor." To this, they assented with enthusiasm, and for once a sight rarely enjoyed by Moses was before Joshua, a united Israel under its leader and under God.

Joshua was a smart, talented and experienced man and one who was not new to the ways of war. All wise warriors, when possible, make a thorough reconnaissance of the impending battlefield. How the memories must have flooded the mind of the now mature and experienced Joshua when he selected two men to "spy secretly" the land of Canaan, even as far as and especially the mighty fortress of Jericho. As a young man Joshua was one of a dozen spies that Moses had sent forth into Canaan, but only he and Caleb returned with a faithful, honest report. Now he dispatched two men, perhaps recalling that the earlier espionage effort failed because of the slackness and faithlessness of ten of the twelve. These two spies, scripturally anonymous, wended their way to Jericho "... and came into a harlot's house, named Rahab and lodged there."

Now, the foundation is being laid for one of the Bible's most interesting and durable stories, that of Rahab "the harlot" followed by the battle of Jericho. Immediately the narrative catches the listener's attention with the awareness that a harlot will be a central character and to many, shockingly, on the side of God and the Israelites. The immediate reason why these two Israelites went to the dwelling of not only a Canaanite harlot, but to employ a name almost of quaintness a "madam" is not known. For one reason or another the men sensed safety at her home, but the king of Jericho displayed an almost mystical knowledge when his messengers pounded on Rahab's door and announced with the almost universal and timeless officiousness and sycophancy of petty bureaucrats:

> "Bring forth the men that are come to thee, which are entered into thine house: for they be come to search out all the country."

Rahab admitted that men had come to her (after all that was her trade and profession) but for the greater good "confessed" that she knew not where they went. Actually, at Rahab's behest the men were lying under heaps of flax upon the roof of her house. Doubtless the Canaanites conducted a search of Rahab's home, and finding no one they departed. They continued their fruitless search far from Rahab's home, as they even crossed the Jordan River in fevered pursuit of the Israelites, who remained still with Rahab, wo now turned to converse and bargain with them.

The men immediately discovered that Rahab was a lady, harlot or not, of historically great character. She was not shy in acknowledging "that the Lord hath given you the land," and in that one phrase Rahab revealed so much of her character.

Steeped in the pagan, polytheistic culture of the Canaanites, unhesitatingly she referred to "the Lord," statement of eloquent simplicity revealing her knowledge that the world was ruled by one God, and one God only, as it was not the pagan stone gods of Baal worship but rather the God of Israel. Still the two Israelite spies doubtless were compelled to ask why that she a woman living a reputably sinful life in the midst of a pagan metropolis would bow down to the God of Moses. Her answer was incredible, and bears praise for the exemplary nature and depth of her faith and understanding. Rahab, a woman of undoubted great presence and strength of character replied:

> "We have heard how the Lord dried up the water of the Red Sea for you when you came out of Egypt; and what you did to the two kings of the Amorites, that were on the other side Jordan, Sihon and Og, whom you utterly destroy."

Two elements of Rahab's faith here meld into one great obelisk of dynamic belief. She recognized strength and power from the knowledge of the recent defeat of the Amorites. Perhaps more jaw dropping is her strong reference to the miraculous parting of the Red Sea. The second is the matter of time and memory. The parting of the Red Sea, to this day the most famous of Old Testament miracles, had not happened the previous week, but was fully over forty years ago! Rehab's age is not known but if living at the time of the great miracle she would have been quite young. Besides, she was a Canaanite, a Gentile, a worshiper of idols. Yet in spite of all this Canaanite woman, through the years, past the ethnic and religious divides acted with knowledge, faith and fear of the God of Israel. Over a millennium later the Savior of all men and women would remark of other Gentile believers that He had never found such faith in Israel as He was shown by believing Gentiles. Rahab was the precursor to such later men and women. Certainly at this time she did not know all the ways of the one true God, but she ordered her own life in belief and faith. How often God must have lamented that He never experienced such faith in all Israel.

Now before the spies fled, they entered into a covenant proposed by Rahab herself:

> "... Save alive my father, and my mother, and my brethren, and all that they have, and deliver our lives from death."

The spies readily assented and agreed that the sign of Rahab and her family would be a scarlet ribbon dangling from the window from which the men escaped. By that thread Rahab and her family would be saved from the onslaught of the Israelite soldiers. The spies escaped and returned to Joshua where they quickly and boldly demonstrated the gritty and optimistic character of Joshua and Caleb rather than the mettle of the ten faithless spies of yore:

> "And they said unto Joshua,
> Truly the Lord hath delivered into our hands all the land; for even all the inhabitants of the country do faint because of us."

What had been promised generations earlier and passed most recently through the hands of Moses and now Joshua, was now at the moment of fulfillment, the entrance of the Chosen into the Promised Land. The entire nation was instructed and organized and led by the priests carrying the ark of the covenant were ready to make a westward crossing of the Jordan River.

Surely the burdens and responsibilities of leadership which weighed so heavily upon Moses were likewise pressing upon the shoulders of Joshua, and the Lord was certainly so aware for He spoke to Joshua:

> "This day will I begin to magnify thee in the sight of all Israel, that they may know, as I was with Moses, so I will be with thee."

How true God was to this statement and with an extraordinarily remarkable symmetry God so demonstrated the truth of His promise. To this day, even into the twenty-first century, as rich and full as was the remarkable life of Moses, to no event is his name more adherent than the parting of the Red Sea. So, Joshua is immediately identified with Moses when now God parts the Jordan River for the Israelites to come in upon dry land. The entire nation so crossed into Canaan in circumstances purposely reminiscent of their ancestors' exodus from Egypt. (Admittedly, though, the Jordan River, famous though it is, remains dwarfed in size by the Red Sea.) The crossing was a marvelous opening to the eventual triumphs which lay ahead, and "... all the people passed clean over."

Jericho

Jericho was one of the oldest and most storied cities of the ancient world. Lying west of the Jordan River about five miles from the river's southernmost fords it was ten miles northwest of the Dead Sea. It was over one thousand feet below sea level making it one of the lowest lying cities in the world. As time progressed it went from a simple agricultural village to a fairly complex urban society, complete with its own king, his army of experienced soldiers and a dense urban environment. Directly to the substance of our narrative, like many, if not most, ancient cities, it was solidly fortified by strong walls which encompassed the city and were constructed to withstand an attack or even a prolonged siege.

Jericho was a very strong point, and it would be a tough opening challenge for Joshua and his Israelite army. The Canaanites had the advantage, always a prized asset militarily, of being on defense, of holding a position against attack. Far from our narrative to offer any real commentary on military strategy and tactics, but for much of history it has been maintained that in customary circumstances a military force requires a three-to-one superiority in men to find success in attack. Also, in the instance of Jericho the city was walled, fortified and constructed to withstand attack by an enemy force. Too, the Canaanites were not neophytes, being practiced, experienced warriors well matched to the Israelites. Israel, though, held an advantage in having placed Jericho under siege, as well described by Joshua in a near perfect definition of "siege":

> "Now Jericho was straitly shut up because of the children of Israel: none went out, and none came in."

Just exactly what was shut and protected behind the walls of Jericho? The city was a jewel of Canaanite civilization, a culture that for this long-ago time was highly advanced and technically proficient. They were advanced in all matters of the arts and sciences, and the Canaanite influence is long lasting, felt even in modern times. They were the ones who developed an alphabet, roughly akin to those of both the Greeks and the Roman Latin, which remains today as the primary Western alphabet. Technologically their weaponry, its construction and design, likely surpassed by many lengths that possessed by the Israelites. Architecturally and with engineering skills they were able to construct a city such as Jericho, far advanced to anything within the grasp of Israel, at this time a wandering, nomadic people. The walled fortifications must have been frightening to any would be assailant, especially a people such as the Israelites, who were still basically inexperienced in the ways of siege craft and war.

All the above catalogue of accomplishments were certainly not to be shrugged off and dismissed, but to God none of these were the main attributes or liabilities of Jericho. This city was a moral cesspool, a running sewer of degradation and likely even a rival to the still infamous Sodom and Gomorrah. Their Baal centered paganism encompassed an endlessly expansive roster of gods and goddesses, very few of whom were represented as having any pretense to kindness and benevolence. It was a center of human sacrifice, even an abundance of child sacrifice to their deity Moloch. They were warlike, aggressive, skillful in battle, but most importantly the Canaanites had a corruptive, even poisonous influence upon the Israelites. God had ordained that Israel neither intermarry with them and essentially to have no dealings with the corrupting Canaanites of any nature. Either they were to be destroyed, or Israel would be destroyed by them. To modern ears especially, such a policy makes many shiver with fright and reproof, but the entirety of the Old Testament would demonstrate that God knew whereof He spoke.

Canaan and its great city Jericho was an evil place to be certain, but it was powerful, quite strong and had the enormous advantage of being on the defensive. Historically, as previously met, the standard rule of thumb is that an attacking force requires at least a three-to-one advantage to enable the defeat of the defender. Logically that ratio is subject to great variance depending upon terrain, topography, the commanders, the soldiers, etc., but the point is well made. Joshua had an army of 40,000 men, many of limited or no experience, to attack a well-fortified large city of a martial people. Could Israel prevail? Perhaps, but perhaps not. The tactics and strategy which Joshua would employ were not those of any military master of antiquity, and would have been incomprehensible by an Alexander the Great or Julius Caesar. Even if the Israelites had been successful, they would have been bathed in blood, likely with casualties so great that the conquest of Canaan would have been delayed. As He so frequently shows, God had another plan, a plan so strange, yet it was a strange simplicity, never known before or since.

Joshua as a general was not totally lacking in assets. At his command was a force of some 40,000 Israelites, a commendably large and noticeable army in any time, place or era. He had the trust and confidence of his fellow Israelites and soldiers, and he well deserved both based upon his exemplary life and successes. Still, before his army marched upon Jericho, Joshua doubtless experienced an entire panoply of emotions, anticipation, dread, fear, self-doubt and endless fraying of his nerves and self-confidence, and so it was all noticed by a stranger. When he was near the famed city Joshua noticed a strange man with a drawn sword in his hand. Joshua walked up to the man and asked the entirely and appropriately relevant question of are "... you for us or for our adversaries?" The man replied with a "nay" and Joshua, as did Moses before him at the Burning Bush:

"...fell on his face to the earth, and did worship
and said unto him,
What saith the Lord unto His servant?"

This man, who identified himself as "captain of the Lord's host" spoke to Joshua the exact words heard by Moses at the Burning Bush:

"Loose thy shoe from off thy foot: for the place
whereon thou standest is holy.
And Joshua did so."

So who was this strange man, the captain of the Lord's host? Our best evidence is from the stories of the scriptures themselves. The testaments record more than one incident where a man bowed down to an angel, and the angel directed him to rise did as when the apostle John fell on his knees before the angel in the Bible's concluding chapter and was told to rise because the angel was John's "fellow servant." Earlier when the Roman centurion Cornelius fell down to worship a man as great as the apostle Peter, Cornelius was told to rise because Peter was "just a man." When Joshua fell on his knees before this man his deference and worshipful attitude were accepted. The captain of the Lord's host must have been the pre-incarnate Jesus Christ himself. In other words the captain of the Lord's host was the Lord Himself.

Still, Jericho remained a fortress city and seemed continually secure in Canaanite hands. Joshua's and Israel's charge was to destroy the defenders, a task still of apparently insurmountable difficulties. Yet, God had promised it to Joshua, with the encouragingly prophetic words that "... I have given unto thine hand Jericho, and the king thereof and the mighty men of valor." What were the strategy and tactics of Joshua which he planned to employ for the destruction of the powerful pagan stronghold? This is a subject to which scholars, historians and generals still devote much of their lives and their thinking, but Joshua, an obviously capable and intelligent man was handed a strategic blueprint by God Himself. It was for a military campaign unlike any seen before and certainly never in the three millennia hence. Its apparent foundation was built upon God's introductory instructions to Joshua that:

> "You shall compass the city, all ye men of war;
> and go round about the city once.
> Thus shalt thou do six days.
>
> And seven priests shall bear before the ark seven trumpets of rams horns."

This opening tactical salvo upon the Canaanites seemingly rested on a capricious foundation of nonsense, yet what followed from God seemed to be even money, blatantly nonsensical:

> "On the seventh day ye shall compass the city seven times, and the priests shall blow with the trumpets.
>
> ,,,(W)hen they make a long blast with the ram's horn, and when ye hear the sound of the trumpet, all the people shall shout with a great shout, and the wall of the city shall fall down flat, and the people shall ascend up every man straight before him."

How fantastic, or as a cynical skeptic would aver, how fanciful that a great city's defenses would fall by such a seemingly whimsical process culminating in a great yell. Yet, this was the God who devastated Egypt with plagues, parted the mighty waters of the Rd Sea and later the Jordan River and fed and watered His people in a desert wilderness for decades. Could He not do this as well?

For six days the Israelite army, with the priest's bearing the ark of the covenant literally "went around in circles" and daily encompassed the great city. We have no record of the observations of the Canaanite spectators, but likely they went through several phases. Initially they were likely puzzled and concerned with the Israelites' strange approach, seeing it as a prelude to some chicanery or strategic trick. During the first days, though, as the army continued marching in circles their enemy likely became a source of amusement, mockery and scorn from the Canaanites. Yet still there was the ominous and totally unworldly silence which finally preyed on Canaanite nerves. The only noise from the Israelites was the daily sounding of their accursed and deplorably abhorrent trumpets, the only noise, that is, until the seventh day.

On that final seventh day the forces of Israel marched around Jericho seven times. Each time, as before, the trumpets blew, but the people were silent until the seventh and final circling. When the trumpets blew this time, the soldiers let out a great shout and thereupon:

> "... the wall fell down flat, so that the people went up into the city, every man straight before him, and they took the city."

As celebrated through the generations in song, rhymes, and inspiring narrative truly did the "walls of Jericho come tumbling down." But this was not the entire story, and the scriptures themselves most eloquently and succinctly tell:

> "They utterly destroyed all that was in the city,
> both man and woman, young and old, and ox,
> and sheep, and ass, with the edge of the sword."

Israel had never won such a victory before. A major city, perhaps even the largest and most important in Canaan had been "utterly destroyed." The city was set ablaze, burned to the ground, and only the gold, silver and brass and non-vessels were salvaged to be placed in the Lord's treasury. The city of Jericho, its very locale, was accursed by God, and at God's behest Jacob pronounced a curse on any man who attempted to rebuild it.

The story of Jericho, its devastation and destruction happily and blessedly ends with an exception. Rahab, the great Canaanite lady, received the total fulfillment of the promise made to her when she rescued the two Jewish spies. She and her entire family were led to safety by the same two men saved by her heroic courage. Married to a man named Salmon she became the mother of Boaz, the husband of the esteemed Moabite woman Ruth. Thus, Rahab was in the lineage of the Savior Himself, that Son of Man from Nazareth, Jesus. As a concluding note we are reminded that the Hebrew translation of Jesus is … Joshua.

CHAPTER TEN

THE SUN STANDS STILL

An old adage, rendered in many fashions and in many languages, proclaims that on the day of victory no one is tired. That being so after the fall of the walls of Jericho and the city's annihilative destruction Joshua and his army must have been a dynamo of energy. Few armies have ever won such a sweeping victory, and none has ever done so in the manner of the Israelites on the day Jericho fell. Under the exceptional and pious leadership of Joshua, Israel had won a victory for the ages. The mighty metropolis of the Canaanites had been utterly ruined, razed to the ground, and its existence mere history. For God had now made it accursed. The city was not to be rebuilt and its ruin to stand as a symbol of the desolation wrought by paganism.

Even the behavior of the Israelites, obedient victors as they were, found itself circumscribed by God's directives. Through Joshua God enunciated what was to be the foundational cornerstone of their conduct:

> "The city shall be accursed, even it, and all that are therein, to the Lord: only Rahab the harlot shall live..."

To God everything about the Canaanites reeked of vileness and moral degradation, and consistent with His desire everything of the Canaanites was "accursed," a term which the scriptural text employs literally. The divine direction began thusly:

> "And you, to any wise keep yourselves from the accursed thing, lest you make yourselves accursed, when yon take of the accursed thing, and make the camp of Israel a curse and trouble it."

So what was this "accursed thing," so frequently noted but never specifically defined? Its broadest definition encompasses all the Canaanite way of life, a life that seemed to be ever aspiring to expand the boundaries of paganism and debauchery. That meant their pagan deities, the grotesque Canaanite worship practices, their manner of thinking and everything about them. God rightly recognized that Canaan itself was an accursed diseased pagan society that could corrupt (and eventually did so in large part) all of Israel. Still with the general guidelines God provided certain specific principles which the Israelites had to follow. God, the Creator, is the source of humanity, and He fully knows its weaknesses and sinful nature. He certainly knew that the proclivity of invading armies is to plunder and loot, subversive to good discipline and quick to turn even a victorious army into a heap of wreckage. Jericho was a city with its share of wealth and the lure of shiny metals such as gold and silver has always stoked the fires of greed in men from the times of Jericho to the twenty-first century. Again, the Israelites had been ordered to abstain from the "accursed thing" and to specify its meaning God ordained:

> "But the silver and gold, and vessels of brass and iron, are consecrated unto the Lord: they shall come into the treasury of the Lord."

Simply stated, fairly stated and easy to understand. None of which, of course, meant that the edict would be meticulously obeyed.

Seemingly Israel had little time to celebrate its great victory until "… the children of Israel committed a trespass in the accursed thing." Certainly no one should deem it shocking that in an army of 40,000 men someone would violate God's specific command. Deplorable, destructive and regrettable but certainly not surprising. The identified culprit was a man named Achan, a member of the tribe of Judah, and "… the anger of the Lord was kindled against the children of Israel." Whether God's anger is a weapon against Israel's collective guilt or just as likely God's knowledge that many of the Israelites wanted to do as Achan, but were not as brazen, is simply not stated. In the meantime, though, the conquest of Canaan was still pending, and the military campaign had to continue at a place with one of the most unique names not only Biblically, but in all history, the city of Ai, which was the next target for Joshua's drive into Canaan.

Ai (Part One)

Now in the third decade of the twenty-first century we are accustomed to seeing the two letters AI juxtaposed one with another. Almost automatically our minds now translate this brief acronym into two words "Artificial Intelligence," a burgeoning technology which as yet no one seems to fully understand.

The original Ai was certainly not artificial, it being a Canaanite settlement on the east of Bethel. Joshua sent men from Jericho to Ai to conduct a reconnaissance, from which they returned with a confident report that Ai was no Jericho, and that it could be easily taken. With an optimism bordering on hubris they counseled Joshua that Israel should save its main army, and that a force of 2,000 to 3,000 men would be sufficient for Ai's conquest.

Joshua chose the route of caution and dispatched 3,000 soldiers to take Ai, a reputedly easy prize to capture. They were wrong, and the Israelite forces never made it past the city gates, where in front of those gates the Canaanites killed thirty-six of the force of Israel before the remainder fled in defeat. The Canaanites pursued, and the Israelite force, was decimated in the ensuing retreat. The proud Israelites, so recently aglow from their great triumph at Jericho, were more than depressed and crestfallen. Beginning with their leader Joshua they acted as if the apocalypse was but a moments distance:

> "And Joshua rent his clothes, and fell to the earth upon his face before the ark of the Lord until the eventide, he and the elders of Israel, and put dust upon their heads."

Joshua's devastation was personal, and he knew the emotional state of his people and that "... the hearts of the people melted as water." He had a demoralized nation, a broken and perhaps even a cowardly army, and the great victories of Israel were now a tormenting personal reminder to him. Joshua fell to the ground, prostrate and wondered what had happened, certainly not the pose and attitude of a great leader. Still, God saw in Joshua just that, a great leader and commanded him to rise from his swamp of despair and resume his duties. As a stern but loving parent God spoke plainly, "no holds barred" with Joshua, but He culminated His instructions with hope and promise. The Lord explained that the children of Israel had "... turned their backs before their enemies, because they were accursed." Starkly God spoke to Joshua, and thus to Israel, that He would abandon him unless they destroyed the accursed this, the private plunder and the manifestation of blatant disobedience.

The following morning Joshua following God's instructions began an investigation into each of the twelve tribes to discover the source of disobedience. He settled upon the largest and ultimately the most prominent and important tribe of Judah and finally winnowed his search down to a man named Achan, the son of Carmi. Achan confessed to the plunder and theft of considerable amounts of silver and gold and other valuables which he had buried by his tent. Joshua's soldiers found the forbidden booty in Achan's tent and brought it to Joshua.

The sad conclusion of Achan's disobedience appears to feature Joshua as the protagonist, but in reality, that role is claimed by God Himself. For well over forty years God had endured the blatant disobedience, the flippant ingratitude and the disloyalty of a people around whom He had built His entire plans for humanity's salvation. He had heard the essentially muted praises of Israel when it chose to worship Him, which often and at the same time their desires and actions were blatantly disobedient. They now were in the midst of one of antiquity's centers of heathenism, and the waves of its idolatry and immorality were always lapping upon the Israelites character. God had determined that any nod to the bacillus which was paganism had to be crushed and eradicated. Od now proclaimed what Anglo-American law would entitle a "bill of attainder" and directed Joshua to assemble not only Achan, his sons, his daughters, all his livestock and all property to the valley of Achor. There all were stoned, and their remains and all the property burned. Idolatry and disobedience would have no place in the Promised Land.

Ai, though, a major impediment remained to be taken.

The Campaign Against Ai (Part Two)

This would be different from Jericho. What's more, God assured Joshua that Ai would be taken, and surprisingly the Israelites were permitted to take the spoils of war and the cattle to themselves.

Joshua had a battle plan that in one form or another has been employed by generals throughout the ages. Knowing that the Canaanites were now secure in a belief that the Israelites were basically cowardly Joshua devised a plan whereby he personally and a small, selected contingent of men would approach the city. When the Canaanites espied them, they would come, attack and pursue Joshua, secure in an already tested belief that the Israelites would run. Joshua, though, had his main army of 30,000 in hiding, ready to destroy the Canaanite forces when they pursued Joshua.

On the morning of anticipated battle Joshua took with him 5,000 men, with the main body of his army hidden west of the city. Joshua's tactics were masterfully executed, and when he and his 5,000 feigned retreat the city of Ai was emptied of defenders as "... not a man left in Ai or Bethel, that went not out after Israel, and they left the city open, and pursued after Israel." At this juncture God directed Joshua to hold forth his spear in the direction of Ai. When he did the Israelite army, hiding in ambush, arose, ran into the city and quickly set it ablaze. In the meantime the men of Ai, all of whom foolishly abandoned the city, were now easy prey for the Israelites "... who smote them so that they let none of them remain or escape."

The Guise of the Gibeonites

From the perspective of the Canaanite enemy Israel's invasion of the Promised Land had premiered as a smashing success for the Israelites and a crushing defeat for the Canaanites. Two of their major cities, Jericho and Ai, already had been cataclysmically destroyed, and they began to ponder what horrors awaited the Canaanite survivors. Canaan, in the aggregate very powerful, was still no centralized state with a king, an emperor, or a common ruler of any sort. They were people united by a common genealogy, a common history and a common culture, but not necessarily any commonality of politics. In this manner and at this time they resembled the ancient Greeks who could achieve unity only upon the threat of a common, powerful enemy at the gates. Now was such a moment. With destruction, even annihilation on the horizon, hastily the Canaanites came together. A conclave of all the rulers and monarchs on the west side of the Jordan River came together to unite in a common effort of defense. This encompassed the entire land westward from the Jordan River to the Mediterranean, and included the rich land of Lebanon, and not only the Canaanites but the Hittites, Perizzites, Hivites, and the Jebusites, by any reckoning a powerful coalition which now "... gathered themselves together to fight with Joshua and with Israel, with one accord." Impressive and inclusive as the alliance was, it was not all inclusive, for among others, a people called the Gibeonites stood outside the circle.

The first scriptural reference to Gibeon appears in this particular story, as the reader finds the Gibeonites pondering and debating the possible means of evading destruction at the hands of the rampaging Israelite army. Evidently, they chose not to join the Canaanite coalition, which was a standard military alliance to repel the invaders, and the usage of such remaining popular and extant yet today (think NATO). The Gibeonites were scared after they witnessed Joshua's thorough destruction. Scared they were, but not scared out of their wits.

For whatever reasons Gibeon had no desire to enter the alliance with the other Canaanites. Neither could little Gibeon hope to stand militarily against a power, Israel, that had already toppled and destroyed two major Canaanite cities. So what were they to do? The pages of the Bible indicate that they chose not the bellicosity of a military alliance or war, but neither would they humiliate (and endanger) themselves with abject surrender. Instead they hoped to win by Canaanite thinking and reasoning against the brutal, bludgeoning tactics of the Israelites. Their plan was both elaborate and ingenious. They would disguise themselves, and the subterfuge of disguise means that a person or people will represent themselves as something they are not. The Book of Joshua itself provides an unequalled narrative, and thus it is quoted:

> "They did work wilily, and went and made as they had been ambassadors, and took old sacks upon their donkeys, and wine bottles, old and rent, and bound up.
>
> And old shoes and clouted upon their feet, and old garments upon them, and all the bread of their provision was dry and mouldy."

In these tattered garbs and all the effects of poor men they rode their donkeys into the Israelite camp at Gilgal and obtained an audience with Joshua and simultaneously declared both their purpose and a proposal:

> "We have come from a far country; now therefore make ye a league with us."

Rapidly their ruse began to unravel. Some of the Israelites spoke up about their immediate recognition that these Hivites were not mysterious ambassadors but rather men that dwelled among the Israelites. Thus, initially they were decidedly wary about making any alliance with them.

Still, the men of Gibeon obtained their meeting with Joshua, where they were only too glad to tell their "story." The explanation of their being present was not preposterous, and like so many falsehoods it contained certain elements of truth. That latter element was encapsulated in one believable declaration to Joshua:

> "From a far country thy servants have come because of the name of the Lord they God for we have heard the fame of Him, and all that He did in Egypt."

The praise of Israel's God was not the finale of the plaudits the Gibeonites laid before Joshua. They continued by explaining that their own leaders had effectively ordered them to prostrate themselves before Joshua as "... (his) servants therefore now make you a league with us." Joshua, an honest man of strength and straightforward ways accepted their offer, made peace and entered into an alliance with them. It would prove to be one of history's shortest-term alliances. After this triad of days the Israelites learned that these putative ambassadors were actually their neighbors. The Israelite forces then went to the three neighboring cities of Gibeon, where undoubtedly all expected violent Israelite retribution for being falsely played.

The violent bloodshed and vengeance came not, as the swords of Israel remain sheathed. The princes and elders, the leaders of Israel forbade vengeance killing "... because the princes of the congregation had sworn unto them by the Lord God of Israel." The Israelites were not happy, but they were assuaged when their princes assured them that though no violent outpouring was allowed the Gibeonites would become their "hewers of wood and drawers of water unto all the congregation, as the princes had promised them."

Finally Joshua himself spoke to the Gibeonites and verbally flailed them for their treachery and imposture. The Gibeonites confessed their fraudulent behavior as well as their fear of Israel and its plans for the Canaanite conquest, and then effectively threw themselves upon the mercies of Joshua. They were unharmed, but their sons and daughters assumed a bonded servitude to Israel.

Gibeon, a mighty city, described as greater than Ai soon would find comfort and salvation in being Israel's ally, even though it was consigned to a decidedly subordinate position. Unfortunately for the Gibeonites being the back end of a new alliance with Israel did not free them from troubles and war. Other lands and the kings of those lands and cities within the Promised Land took notice of this radical change in the political dynamics of Canaan. Gibeon, an assumedly and noteworthy strong power had made peace with Israel and had crossed the line to the other side. Not why did the military situation but also the emotional shock called for a stark and dramatic response from the Canaanites and their allies. Adoni-zedek, king of Jerusalem, at the time a Jebusite fortress but later to become the most storied city in history, contacted Hoham, king of Hebron, Japhia, king of Lachesh and Debir, king of Eglon and proclaimed to his fellow monarchs:

> "Come up unto me, and help me, that we may smite Gibeon: for it hath made peace with Joshua and with the children of Israel."

Thus began the coalescence of the five kings, each a ruler of a city-state of potency, into a military alliance to destroy not Israel (which would come later) but rather their own turncoat erstwhile ally Gibeon. So, they "and all their hosts... encamped before Gibeon and made war against it."

Quickly Gibeon turned to Israel, a newly minted but strange combination of master and ally, and sought rescue from the aid of Joshua and his army. Joshua was true to the alliance and came from Gilgal with "... all the mighty men of valor" to confront the armies of the five kings and save Gibeon. On its face and its factual backdrop, this would be no walkover, no snap decision, but God was true to Joshua and the chosen Israelites, as He told Joshua:

> "(F)ear them not; for I have delivered them unto thine hand: there shall not a man of them stand before thee."

True to His promise God visited upon the Five Kings a great "slaughter," not only in Gibeon but also in the cities to which they attempted to flee.

The believer sees throughout both Testaments that God acts in many ways to perform His will. So often it is done indirectly, as this current example of Joshua so aptly demonstrates, but often quite directly from His own Hand. After all it was not Moses who parted the Red Sea, and to cite a later famous example it was not the great prophet Elijah who directly sent down the fire upon Mount Carmel. Neither was it Joshua but rather God who would be the primary victor over the Five Kings.

Many escaped from the battle at Gibeon, and they had become a desperate mob in flight from a victorious enemy. In flight they were, but it was a path to their own doom:

"(A)s they fled from before Israel, and were in the going down to Beth-honor, that the Lord cast down great stones from heaven and upon them unto Azekah, and they died: they were more which died with hailstones than they whom the children of Israel slew with the sword."

A fairly common expression always has been to remark about a particularly eventful and historic day that "this is a day like no other." It is a pity that like most common expressions this one has been worn down by overuse, and in our present narrative its too frequent application somewhat diminishes this day on which Joshua and Israel defeated the five Kings. This was the day, as proclaimed by scripture, truly like no other before or since.

The Sun Stands Still

The Amorite kings remained alive and free, and Joshua needed time to reach them. It is endemic to the human being to think and always plead for "more time" to accomplish a task, yet humanity has yet (and never will) find a method to enlarge or expand time. Yet with man what is impossible is possible with God. Plainly and without any ornamentation or fanfare the text records"

> "Then spake Joshua to the Lord in the day when the Lord delivered up the Amorites to the children of Israel, Sun, stand thou still upon Gibeon; and thou Moon, in the valley of Ajalon.
>
> And the sun stood still, and the moon stayed, until the people had avenged themselves upon their enemies."

This was a day of true singularity and so the scriptures expressed that "... there was no day like that before it or after it" where "...the sun still in the midst of heaven, and hasted not to go down upon a whole day."

How often in history would a general have begged for just a few hours more or daylight to accomplish his attack or before, but always the sun "rises" and "sets" according to Divinely predetermined times. Yet the earth promptly returned to its normal speed of rotation and revolution, and daylight and dark returned to their normal order. For, the victory of Joshua and Israelites was truly earned and miraculous, but one turn was left undone. The Five Kings of the Amorites had escaped and fled to a cave in a locale called Makkedah. Already a military leader who thought and acted quickly he dispatched some men to Makkedah with a directive to roll great stones and temporarily seal this cavernous hiding place of the Five Kings. Thus his soldiers did.

Another indicia of the growing greatness of Joshua as a general was his desire to be absolutely thorough. He knew that many Amorite soldiers remained and that they continued to conduct a type of rear-guard action against Israel. Joshua thus gave the command for the Israelite forces to pursue and destroy these remnants of the Amorite foe, and thus they did. In the starkness of Old Testament language, a means which hides not the often-grim reality of truth it was recorded that:

> "When Joshua and the children of Israel had made an ending of slaying (the Amorites) with a very great slaughter, till they were consumed, and the rest which remained of them entered into fenced cities."

Israel had won a victory of astonishing proportion and thoroughness so that at the end "... none moved his tongue against any of the children of Israel."

As for the Five Kings, Joshua himself went to the enclosing cave and ordered the stone removed. The leader of Israel then engaged in what his detractors might call theatrics, but which was likely meant as a Divine symbol and portent to all of God's own plans for Israel. Joshua was now the general manager of trifecta of victories over Jericho, Ai and the Five Kings, and by his brilliant obedience to God's commands his reputation and admiration were resting upon a pinnacle of achievement. He called forth his subordinate officers, the captains of his soldiers, where Joshua stood with an assemblage of the vanquished Amorite kings. Following ancient customs and traditions he had his captains literally place their feet upon the necks of the kings lying prostrate before them. Joshua spoke before victor and vanquished the meaning of this symbolic humiliation when he spoke:

> "Fear not, nor be dismayed, be strong and of good courage: for thus shall the Lord do to all your enemies against whom ye fight."

The lesson to be learned, and which every unlearned by the Israelites under Moses was expressed by Joshua:

> "Fear not, nor be dismayed, be strong and of good courage: for thus shall the Lord do to all your enemies against whom ye fight."

The Five Kings, monarchs so powerful in their day and their place later that evening were taken down from the trees on which they were hanged, their bodies cast into the cave in which they hid, and the stone rolled onto its entrance, where it was recorded, they "... remain until this very day."

In a relatively short span of time Joshua (to be properly understood as "God with us") had become a strong, mighty and reliable ruler and general. His selection as the successor to Moses well belied the Divine ability to find the right person for the moment. In succession Joshua had defeated and razed the fortress city of Jericho, had destroyed the city of Ai, and smashed the power of the Five Kings of the Amorites. None of this was done in secrecy or silence and it was not accomplished without blood, copious quantities of blood, casualty lists of gargantuan proportions and the ongoing destruction of a culture and civilization. Joshua had what had developed into a dynamic engine of power, the army of the Israelites, and its every movement was at his command. The reasons for the slaughter and bloodshed will be more fully explored in Chapter Ten, but for now we posit it as a factual foundation. Joshua was a powerful man, whose power was demonstrated before the commencement of battles. He had parted the Jordan River and later famously ordered the sun to "stand still" for a day. Yet the Biblical text, which is thorough, never indicates that Joshua himself boasted of power, saw it as his self-generated within his own character. Over one millennia later in what was a portion of the Promised Land another man from a small, obscure and rather opprobrious village would more perfectly (actually with true perfection) demonstrate real power on earth and in heaven, but power in a different manner.

This man, now known in a later time by the Greek version of Joshua, i.e. Jesus, was with that group of men who were His closest disciples and later His apostles one night on the Sea of Galilee, actually a small freshwater lake in Galilee, when a storm arose, and the winds and waves battered the little boat on which they were all being tossed about. These were experienced fishermen, who knew the fears engendered by the winds and the water, which now filled their frail craft and filled their hearts with the fears of sinking and drowning. Jesus, though, lay asleep, and frantically did his disciples wake Him with the rebuke of "Master, carest thou not that we perish?" He stood, rebuked the wind and spoke to the waters those beautiful words of life-giving serenity:

> "Peace, be still. And the wind ceased, and there was a great clam."

The disciples were not to be drowned in water, but they were immersed in the emotions of fear, wonder, relief and pure astonishment when they exclaimed "what manner of man is this that even the winds and the sea obey Him?" The Joshua of Israel had power entrusted to him by God, and he invariably employed it wisely and without personal vainglory. It was God's power, though, and so Joshua knew it. Undoubtedly, he took no pleasure in the bloodshed and carnage that often resulted from its use. The Joshua of the New Testament, Jesus

Christ, had "all power in heaven and earth given to Him," and He remains known as the Prince of Peace.

Joshua and Israel had done very well in the beginning of their campaigns. In fact they enjoyed success of superlative proportions. Still, Joshua had many miles to travel before peace awaited him and his people. They now drove forward deeper into Canaan to meet their fate.

CHAPTER ELEVEN

PARADISE LOST

In his epic poem "Paradise Lost," one of the foundational blocks of Western civilization, the seventeenth century English Puritan poet, wrote in his work's opening stanza that "I may assert Providence, and justify the ways of God to men." John Milton, a phenomenally unique talent of theological insight and literary magnetism that it yet remains influential. If any man or woman possessed the mental breadth and acumen to "justify" God it was Milton, but such talents have not been vested in the author. What is more to the point is that to the believer God requires no justification or explanation, for He remains as He told Moses "I am that I am." The first sentence of the Bible proclaims in its fourth word "In the beginning God..." Thereafter He is taken as absolute, omniscient, omnipotent and omnipresent. He needs not our feeble attempts at justification, but perhaps at times it could aid our understanding of Him, and both learned and explained His ways, at least to the extent that they have been revealed to us.

So often, especially in modern times, have questions been raised about the justification and legitimacy of Israel's conquest of the Promised Land. The Biblical record in the Book of Joshua leaves little room for conjecture and/or debate. It must be clear to all readers, of whatever persuasion and belief, that the conquest of Canaan was extraordinarily violent and bloody. Too, to the interested and knowledge seeking observer it appears to them so often that Israel's invasion and destruction was wholly unjustified, and that Israel attacked, butchered and destroyed wholly without provocation. These questions are not necessarily a display of faithlessness or skepticism (though sometimes they are) but rather an attempt to reconcile the actions of a Father who later gave the world Jesus Christ, a man described so gentle that "He would not break a bruised reed" who had earlier commissioned Joshua to wage a seemingly unprovoked war upon the inhabitants of the Promised Land?

This world that the Almighty has created has been since the Fall a realm of unremitting violence, at times so extreme that humanity seemed forsworn to destroy itself. An activity so large and encompassingly monstrous as war is bound to produce anomalies of the strangest sort that in spite of their horrors tend to be irresistible to our attention. As we meander more deeply into the twenty-first century it may be helpful to re-examine that greatest of all human conflicts, World War II, the one hundredth anniversary of which, is just beyond our horizon. Its weaponry and its destructiveness, the overall casualty rate and its terrors are historical but remain beyond a certain human comprehension. The mechanisms for killing had developed so that death could come from a distance. From several miles above the earth airplanes dropped bombs upon targets that had been identified through mechanical devices, effective though they were, that now seem primitive. Artillery pieces, usually several miles behind the front, found the range of the enemy's lines and visited upon them more death from afar. Massive naval warships exchanged salvos of destruction from huge guns rarely seen by the enemy's forces. All this and more accounted for the overwhelming majority of deaths to both soldier and civilian. It is not uncommon, especially in histories of the European theater, to find that the memories and accounts of many veteran soldiers speak of the phenomenon of never actually seeing their enemy counterpart, be he American, German, British, or otherwise. Killing was done under a shroud of anonymity. On the other hand...

The battlefields of antiquity were charnel horses of slaughter, wherein the soldier looked his enemy in the eye while trying to take his life. Long before the invention of high explosives and the weaponry propelled by its power, battlefield killing was highly personal. Depending upon the time and place the typical combatant carried a roughly hewn "edged" weapon, generally a sword, but for all practical purposes an elongated knife or dagger. The soldier would hopefully block and parry with his shield the blows of his foes and then plunge the roughly sharpened and crudely fashioned sword into the vital organs of his enemy. Perhaps if his haste and the development of the combat dictated with a hacking motion, he would sever the arm or hand, in some rare instances even the decapitation of his enemy. The blood and body matter would gush and flow profusely. It was a horrid, hellish process that only the most brutish could savor. This was a snapshot into ancient combat.

All of this, though, is a description, albeit horribly macabre, of ancient combat between two equal soldiers meeting man-to-man. We are compelled to imagine if that soldier's victim was not a trained soldier, but a civilian not inured to the ways of battle. Now the sword is plunged into the body of a woman, an older lady of no threat to anyone, or a mother of several children or even a lovely young girl in the prime of her beauty. Ultimately, our roll call of examples reaches the child or an infant whose life is brutally extinguished before it has really begun. All this is what the soldiers of Joshua, the Israelites, the Chosen, did at Jericho, Ai and the Battle of the Five Kings. It was all done at the direction of God, the God who is ever proclaimed as the God of love. Why? How?

The Promised Land, still known historically and presently by so many names, was not the land of the Canaanites, the Annalikites, the Amorites or any of the other multitudes of enemies of Israel. It was the land promised by God to Abraham, Isaac and Jacob (a/k/a Israel) and for our purposes now to be called Israel. As we go deeper into modernity it is now claimed by the descendants of many of these same people, including the ethnic descendants of Israel's three great named patriarchs. Israel was the land promised to the Hebrew people from the days of Abraham and as renewed during the depths of the degradation of Egyptian slavery to Moses. It was always meant to be Israel's, not those of any Gentile interlopers and trespassers. The land, actually quite small in area, was meant to be Israel's, but the greater eternal plans were for the Israelites as God's Chosen. God's intention, set forth meticulously in the Old (and New) Testaments was for the Hebrews to have the land and be set apart from the Gentile world. At this point in Biblical history God did not necessarily wish for Jew and Gentile to coexist, but not because the Israelites were inherently and intrinsically better than the Gentiles. They could not coexist and intermingle, especially at this still early stage of Israel's history, not because of what the Jews would do to the Canaanites but because of the damage and destruction the Canaanites would wreak upon the Israelites, physically but most of all spiritually.

At this point in history the Gentile world was one that "dwelled in darkness" and upon which no light had yet shone. Its gods were Mammon (materiality) and for the Canaanites an entire panoply of false deities under the great god Baal. The gods and goddesses, much like the later Western and classical deities of Greece and Rome, actually seemed to be more human than human beings themselves. The deities of the Canaanites, by some estimates, exceeded two thousand in numbers, and for every little action or aspect of life a god existed. It is subject to an easily drafted essay to write and opine upon the monstrosity of the Canaanite religion from child sacrifices to sadistic torture, but we rely upon the interest of the individual reader to pursue such privately. Unfortunately it remains to note that the Canaanite religion and especially their multitudes of individual gods and goddesses was awash with human sexuality, not just that which could fit comfortably within "normality" but sadism, masochism, torture and human sacrifice. Even many of their deities were represented in animate form as human sexual genitalia. From infancy the Canaanite culture was immersed and ensnared in activity that can be aptly described with no other word than Satanic.

The Canaanites and their allies often were aggressive and expansive with their power, their culture and their perverted morality. God, the Creator of both Canaan and Israel knew what would (and most often did) happen when His people existed, commingled and intermarried with the Canaanites. Either the Canaanites were pushed back with a seemingly ferocious brutality, or the nascent nation of Israel would be culturally and spiritually destroyed in the veritable cradle of its existence. Canaan was capable of conquest, but at this time in history not of conversion. For the sake of His own children the Canaanites and their allies were dealt a ruthless, even brutal punishment by Joshua and his soldiers. The consequences of their failure would be even more abhorrent. This does not remain speculative, but unfortunately turns into the very spine of most of the Old Testament historical chronicles.

God blessed Israel greatly, but He above all certainly knew the demonstrated weaknesses of His Chosen. A rehash of Israel's history is unnecessary and would be tedious but suffice it for the moment to understand that Israel's faith and devotion to God had always been weak or even non-existent. God's plan of winnowing away by time and death the original generations which had left the shackles of Egyptian slavery was working. His chosen leader, Joshua, had at his command now a large veteran army of experienced, battle tested soldiers, likely the equal man-for-man of army force it would encounter. Militarily, the building and at time the revitalization of Israel's military forces had been a shining success, yet the deeper character of Israel's new generation had still to be fully tested. Undoubtedly, God knew that its mixture and even intermarriage with the Canaanite inhabitants of the land would be the moral equivalent of an injection of deadly poison into the spiritual bloodstream.

Some twelve hundred years later the great minister of Christ, the apostle Paul, rhetorically posed the question of "... what communion has light with darkness." None, of course, and neither were the Israelites to have such dealings with the inhabitants of the Promised Land, the Canaanites and their allies. Any but a cynic or a skeptic can accept this reasoning. No matter how skillfully the "justification" of God's actions in killing the Canaanites in Jericho, Ai and other sites may be presented, at base the reluctant or even the reluctant believer may still ask why was the bloodshed Divinely necessary. In this matter perhaps the so-called "justification" of God's actions rests upon a dual foundation. The first stone of that foundation has been examined, and in the tersest of terms it was "kill or be killed," the Israelites or the Canaanites. But any reasonable observer, attuned to a non-violent life and the protection of the weak and defenseless still asks, both in wonder and somewhat in horror "...but children?" This path of reasoned inquiry leads directly to the second of God's reasons, or at least those which we can ascertain and identify.

Long established Christian doctrine is that the souls of children are vouchsafed in Heaven by God through the redemption of Christ. Those Canaanite children who grew up nurtured and force-fed paganistic propaganda and idolatry would have grown to be as contemptable adults as were those who raised them. They possessed no other alternatives. An early exit from this world into the arms of the Savior was their lot. The faithless and the atheist, the ancient and the modern, are welcome to scorn this reasoning, but its source is the well documented and told plan of Redemption. Growing and maturing in paganistic Canaanite idolatry was spiritual and eternal death.

Neither a participant, a victim, nor an interested historical observer could reasonably deny that the Israelite conquest of Canaan was anything short of brutal and bloody. These descendants of Abraham, Isaac and Jacob, had been marked by God as His Chosen, and His intention was that they prevail. Unless the Canaanites were destroyed, the Israelites would be destroyed by the Canaanites. As the record will show and likewise our brief summary the end result was a hodgepodge, a strange historical and spiritual compromise between the pagans of Canaan and the Chosen Israelites led by Joshua.

Our narrative will now proceed and will reflect that the Israelites conquered the Promised Land, but they neither eradicated paganism, nor its Canaanite devotees. Ultimately (and we hope that we are not getting ahead of ourselves) much of Israel was infected by the heathen way of life, and the lion's share of this already small nation would be swallowed and destroyed by the pagans who they were commissioned by God to conquer. We defer a thorough discussion of the fate of most of Israel to a later chapter. For now, though, it must be admitted sadly that God's plans and hopes to guard most of Israel from Canaanite idolatry after a few generations collapsed in obloquy and failure to where only a frail fragment of the descendants of Abraham even survived.

The great Athenian philosopher Plato once remarked that "... only the dead have seen the end of war." As profound as this great Greek thinker could be his remark was later placed in the shadows when a far greater remarked that "... there shall always be wars and rumors of wars." So it remained to Israel. The conquest which had begun with a flood of blood upon the land would continue. Joshua was becoming a great general and a great leader, and he was leading a battle tested soldiery. Still, before any conquest could be called complete battles remained to be fought.

CHAPTER TWELVE

THE LAND THAT WAS PROMISED

Rivers, torrents, waves of blood had already cascaded across the plains and down the hills of southern Canaan. Most of the blood had been that of the Canaanites and their allies, but the army of Israel had suffered. At the will and under the Providence of God the army of Israel had conquered and destroyed the primary fortresses of the south, namely Jericho, Ai and Gibeon. Tens of thousands had lost their lives and to a large extent Israel could be relieved that the southern portion of the Promised Land, or at least its urban citadels of southern Canaan. While this was literally a Divinely directed campaign with that specific result as its purpose untold numbers of Canaanites and Gentiles remained in the south, in other towns, villages and in the rural hinterland. The brittle old adage is that to the victor belong the spoils of war, and for this brief narrative we claim one. This is a small sliver of land on the coast of the eastern Mediterranean Sea, which was and yet remains known by many names, almost all disputed. They include Canaan, the Promised Land, the Levant, later the northern and the southern kingdoms, but for now its immediate reference shall be Israel, the most common name historically, given in honor of the descendants of Israel (a/k/a Jacob). Should the context call for another sobriquet it will be offered, but for the present the scene of action is "Israel."

Should one say "southern" kingdom the remaining clear implication is that a "northern" kingdom must be considered and construed. So shall it be as the stage is moved to northern Israel. The north, generally more temperate and lush than the south, was a prosperous place of undetermined population and one which the Israelites sorely wanted and needed. Now, over three millennia into the future we should not attempt to overly describe ancient Canaan and Israel with what are essentially more modern geopolitical concepts. Much as an ancient land more familiar to modern observers (or at least once so), ancient Greece it was a place with no central authority, but an abundance of what the Greeks called city-states. These were independent municipalities, each autonomous and separately governed whose authority extended but little beyond its own city boundaries. No central authority existed, but the cities and their kings often formed alliances for common purposes and for common foes. No better or more distinct example may be found than in a crisis now facing the Canaanites of the north. They knew that their neighbors, brothers and sisters in the south had been devastated and decimated by these strange invaders and interlopers from the west. To the Canaanites, whatever else they might be, they had already proven to the rulers, men and women of Canaan that as God's Chosen, the Israelites, they were a deadly force to be considered.

Safety in numbers is the old adage. Another such, not quite as old or revered is that the only thing worse than fighting a war with allies is fighting one without allies. The most prominent northern Canaanite king, a man named Jabin, king of Hazor, obviously believed in the efficacy of this truism. Jabin, like any good leader, was well apprised of the situation, and he knew that in the absence of a coalition, an alliance, a league, or whatever, the Canaanite city-states of the north were easy prey to be picked off one-by-one by these ruthless invaders under Joshua. Jabin himself must have possessed a fair amount of leadership qualities and initiative, for soon he had assembled a coalition which included Jobab, king of Madon, and the various kings and generals of Kinnereth (or Galilee) and to people than Canaanites, including the Amorites, the Hittites and the Perizzites. So great was their assembly with all their populations and warriors that the chronicler of these events, Joshua himself, employed a phrase originally uttered by God Himself who attempted to describe the vastness of the numbers of Abraham's descendants. John and his allies are described as:

> "... much people, even as the sand that is upon the seashore in multitude, with horses and chariots very many."

That one brief sentence expresses the formidability of the enemy which was prepared to face Joshua's forces in battle. The number of his soldiers is not specifically reckoned, though it must have been impressive because of its metaphorical description. At his command Jabin also had cavalry, so important in pre-modern combat, but the scriptures are silent on whether the Israelites had similar forces. The chances are that they did not. The Chariots, frightening machines of war not easily stopped or even slowed by infantry soldiers, may be considered as antiquity's equivalent of a modern armored force of tanks and other armed fighting vehicles. To this awesome, apparently united array of military forces Joshua could present a large force of now highly experienced and victorious foot soldiers, men and officers who rightly had confidence in Joshua and hopefully in the God of Israel.

As to finding any specificity in the numbers of combat soldiers on either side of this conflict, we must, as best, come to an educated guess. Canaan was a well populated land even in ancient time with an apparently organized military system which included a multiple of the combat arms. It was well organized, experienced and seems to have been under the direction of localized kings who had no difficulty in coordinating their efforts and to whom the others would not be excessively jealous if one were granted temporary power over the others. Militarily, for the times it was an advanced culture of intelligent people with a multi-generational history of successful military campaigns. An estimate of 50,000 soldiers taking the field does not seem an exaggeration, although no one can state for sure. Besides, they were defending their homes, their lives, their families and their religion, with all the heathen gods and goddesses anyone could desire. They were defending their "hearth and home" and promised to be an enemy of extreme formidability.

The Israelites were different. Though it may seem otherwise they were not martial or warlike in their nature. Yet time, a great leader in Joshua, experience and the pleasure and desires of the Divine had inculcated in them skills which had produced great, historic and massive histories. When the two enemies, Gentile and Jew, pagan and God fearing, attacked and attacker, met a day of bloody, sanguinary combat was promised and all but assured. That great day of unmatched drama, of two great armies staring at each other before honing in on the foe's destruction never came. This conflict between Israel and the northern Canaanites did not crescendo into a dramatic moment such as Waterloo or

Gettysburg where two well matched forces stared at each other across peaceful terrain before engaging in conflict of unparalleled and continuously chronicled drama. The God of Heaven had invested into Joshua the knowledge and wherewithal to attain victory, a total victory, in another manner.

As our story has been told the Canaanites had multiple advantages over Joshua's Israelites, but in a technical and purely military sense two stood over and above the others, those being their possession of cavalry and chariots, the skillful employment of which would negate any possible advantages the experienced Israelite infantry could claim. At the behest and direction of Israel's God the odds were about to be evened, and such was to be accomplished without the shooting of an arrow or the swinging of a sword. Great was the number of the Canaanite cities and their armies which faced Israel. Even greater, though, was the generalship of Joshua under the Divine Hand of God, as Joshua began gradually to destroy the Canaanites in detail. Joshua attacked their cities and armies of Zidon, Misrephoth-maim and Mizpah and won victories great for Israel and calamitous for the Canaanites. Yet Joshua was not fighting their armies at the zenith of their strength and power, but rather the forces of an energy weakened by the direction of God. While the Biblical text does not provide a narrative of the time, place or manner in which the acts were done, it plainly states:

> "Joshua did unto them as the Lord bade him: he houghed (hamstrung) their horses and burnt their chariots with fire."

The advantage enjoyed by the Canaanites had been displaced by the strategies of God and the brilliant obedience of Joshua.

Suddenly and by subterfuge the military advantages enjoyed by the Canaanites had evaporated.

Again, a terrible fate awaited the Canaanites, their cities and their leaders, and the victory of Israel was made historic for:

> "Joshua at that time turned back and took Hazor and smote the king thereof with the sword: for Hazor beforetime was the head of all those kingdoms.
>
> And they smote all the souls that were therein with the edge of the sword, utterly destroying them; there was not any left to breathe: and he burnt Hazor to the ground."

The cities of the Canaanites, Amorites, Hivites, Jebusites had been utterly destroyed, razed to the ground and were smoldering ash heaps and ruins. The conquest of the cities had not been pleasant, but the spine of Israel had been stiffened. In Joshua God had found, although we are hesitant to employ the term the "perfect" leader. Certainly he was not perfect or sinless in moral terms, for he was a man as other men, but "perfect" in an older commonly accepted use of the word as "complete." He was a wellspring of strength to all, especially all those younger Israelites who had not suffered the shackles of Egyptian slavery and many who had endured no years of wilderness wanderings. His people, at least who were sensitive in any manner to their nation's own history were aware of the importance of Joshua's own heritage, that he had been the strong right of arm of none other than Moses, the most revered of all men.

The God of Israel, Moses and Joshua, the same who remains the God of all has always sought perfection. He above all knows that true perfection can come through His own Son, Jesus Christ, whose earthly appearance came not for centuries to come. Yet God sought and still seeks perfection in all men and women, but more realistically in the absence of Christ the "perfection" as was more commonly understood in our English language of several centuries ago. It is the "perfection" of thoroughness and completion, the attentive, at times intense devotion to life in general and to the tasks of the moment specifically. In this, his servant Joshua had proven perfectly complete and magnificently so. The scriptures of the Lord are not hesitant in their praise for this man:

> "As the Lord commanded Moses His servant, so did Moses command Joshua, and so did Joshua he left nothing undone of all that the Lord commanded Moses."

The accomplishments of Joshua as general and leader remain awe-inspiring, and just their mere recitation so proves. Joshua by his steadfast service and brilliant obedience to God had secured the Promised Land, now Israel, but it had been no bloodless walkover for the Israelites and most certainly not the Canaanites.

It all came at a price, a large, burgeoning cost for both Israel and Canaan and its allies. Israel's victory had been sweeping, far-flung, and sanguinary. Yet it was not total, even in a strict military sense. Joshua had taken the land of Goshen from whence many of the Israelites originally had lived while in Egyptian slavery, "... and the valley, and the plain, and the mountain of Israel." Again, the scriptures provide a coda, a result of the thoroughness of the battles and victories of Israel:

> "Even from the mount Halak, that goeth to Sier, even unto Baal-gad in the valley of Lebanon under mount Hermon: and all their kings he took, and smote them, and slew them."

The Canaanites assuredly were a belligerent, skillful and brave foe. Every city, save Gibeon and its inhabitants the Hivites, refused peace, so all were taken and killed. In the eloquent simplicity of the Bible "Joshua made war a long time with those kings."

Many were the names and ethnology of the people of Israel when Joshua began to decimate their cities. Their reactions to Israel's coming probably to an opening of their eyes to the character of this surprisingly strong antagonist, Israel, with their strange ways and even stranger God. One enemy of substance remained in Israel's path to total victory and conquest. A people called the Anakins were spread throughout the land. They lived in the mountains of Hebron, Debir and Ana. All the way south into mountainous regions of Judah. More Israelite success awaited, and the cities of the Anakins were destroyed, and they remained only in three cities of the west, Ashdod, Gaza and Gath (from which more later).

So Joshua had taken the entire Promised Land, the pledges and promises of God having been fulfilled. Temporarily the chronicles rest from blood and destruction with the blessed words "... And the land rested from war." The "Promised" Land was no longer a mysterious chimera set before the Israelites, for the promise of its realization had now come to pass. From the time God first spoke to Moses from the Burning Bush on Sinai many decades had elapsed. The national life of Israel had been harsh, but finally the land flowing with milk and honey was theirs. So what would they do with it, and who would lead them? Joshua was old and had lived and at times endured a harsh life of deprivations and was, yet must strenuous work remained to be done. For now, Israel possessed land and a leader, but for the moment they were a new people in a land unknown to them. Daily life, business, agricultural and all the other often overlooked essentials of life demanded consideration and processing. For that matter God told the aged Joshua that:

> "Thou art old and stricken in years, and there remaineth very much land to be possessed.
> This is the land that yet remaineth: All the borders of the Philistines, and all Gershom."

He then expanded on His narrative to Joshua that many lands remained to be taken from a miscellany of Gentile nations whose names begin to run together to any but the most astute and dedicated Biblical scholar. The most prominent of these were the Philistines, the hill country inhabitants of Lebanon (later to be historically known as the Phoenicians) and vast numbers of Canaanites still remaining.

Already God began to direct an organized and detailed division of Israel, and He effectively directed the platting and subdivision of the lands to the various tribes. The Lord acknowledged that Moses had already directed the tribes of Reuben, Gad and half the tribe of Manasseh to have the territory east of the Jordan River, and so He ratified that assignment. This grouping and location of these tribes is not without a certain, even great, import in the future history of Israel. While it remains a factor in modernity in the antiquity of which we study geography could achieve an outsized importance. These three tribes were separated from the remainder of Israel by the Jordan River, itself by means of a major waterway, but still a barrier of separation from the bulk of the nation. These people developed their culture separate and apart from the mainstream of Israel. They remained Israelites, but proved to be especially prone to the corruption of Gentile influences, especially paganism, which continually pressed upon them. Although by no means a singular phenomenon Reuben, Gad and the half tribe of Manasseh developed a certain aberration from the main body of Israel, and they were to be seen in the vanguard of future decline and collapse.

Upon initial inspection the distribution of the shares of Israel to the remaining nine and one-half tribes seems odd and even somewhat in conflict with the peculiar status of Israel as God's Chosen people. Our account succinctly states:

> "By lot was their inheritance, as the Lord commanded by the hand of Moses, for the nine tribes and for the half tribe."

Employing the phrase "by lot" Biblically and with reasonable logic forces the reader to think of the later macabre scene on Calvary where the Roman soldiers cast lots for the garments of the crucified Savior. Moreover, the morality of the Bible has consistently taught against gambling per se as sin. This was not to be gambling, though, but rather the casting of lots would serve as a type of declaration and proclamation of God for the division and allocation of the land. In total twelve of the thirteen tribes, representing the twelve sons of Jacob would participate. One tribe, that of Levi, would receive no specific allocation of land, not because of any sin or misdeed but rather because the Levites would be the priests and the religious leaders of the people, and as God explained:

> "(T)herefore they gave no part unto the Levites in the land, save cities to dwell in, with their suburbs for their cattle for their substance."

With the tribe of Levi's special status and assignment to retain the almost sacred number of twelve another tribe and another son were needed. God's methodology, though, was a bit different. By far the most prominent of Jacob's sons and a man of lasting, even eternal fame was Joseph, yet one never speaks of the tribe of Joseph, a non-existent entity. Instead, God honored this magnificent man by providing two tribes from Joseph's lineage, named after his two sons, Manasseh and Ephraim.

Before the narrative proceeds with the putatively dreary subject of land allotment (certainly more important and hopefully more interesting than its reputation) a name from the past must be recalled as that of Caleb. This is the man, along with Joshua, one of the two believing adult Israelites, who forty-five years earlier had been the two spies who possessed faith that Israel could conquer Canaan. Now, much later these two great servants, Joshua and Caleb, reconvened and Caleb, now 85 assured Joshua that he was a strong as he had been "in the day of Moses." As his share of the land Caleb requested from Joshua the mount of Hebron, and gladly Joshua so acceded. Well deserved it was for Caleb, a man described as one "... who wholly followed the God of Israel."

God now directed His plans towards the division and His conveyancing of the remainder of the land to the remaining tribes, and fittingly the first to be discussed were the sons of Jospeh. Half of Manasseh's allotment, as has been noted, lay east of the Jordan River. The other half of Manasseh received a squarish allotment on the west of the Jordan stretching to the Mediterranean coast. Although it is not yet relevant to the story it may be noted that centuries later, after wars, calamities, political upheavals and revolutions, this geographical block of land became the heart of a land so important in the New Testament, Samaria.

Ephraim, the "brother" tribe of Manasseh was given the relatively small portion of land immediately south and adjacent to the western half of Manasseh. Both Manasseh and Ephraim resented the perceived paucity of their allotments and complained to Joshua, saying:

> "Why hast thou given me but one lot and one portion to inherit, seeing I am a great people, forasmuch as the Lord has blessed me hitherto?"

These descendants of the great Joseph, obviously aware of their self-presumed special status, were so enamored with their bloodlines that they demanded even more from Joshua. So consumed with their self-identity they spoke of themselves in the first person "I" in an obvious assertion of their unity with Joseph. We may well observe that the passage of centuries and even millennia has in no wise drilled the senses of many persons to still claim rights and standing based upon the deeds and character of ancestors from many generations earlier. Joshua, as reasonable and equitable leader as could be found, did not recoil at the demands of these remote ancestors of the storied Joseph. In fact, he agreed with them, readily conceding as:

> "Joshua spoke unto the house of Joseph, even to Ephraim and to Manasseh, saying thou art a great people, and hast great power; thou shalt not have one lot only."

Joshua added to their allotment a mountainous, wooded area; however, as if to prove that the old adage of "be careful what you wish for you may get it" it was on the presupposition that they would cut down the woods "... for thou shalt drive out the Canaanites, though they have iron chariots, and though they be strong." This added allotment was in the middle of Canaanite strength and power, a force that had yet to be fully subdued by Israel. These two tribes, glorious though their ancestry be, were handed great responsibility along with their promised land.

Of course the other tribes were not forgotten and were not short changed. These included those of Simeon, which received the southernmost allotment, Zebulon, Issachar, Asher, Dan and Naphtali. Each had its own history and future, which deserves retelling, but for the moment our narrative moves forward. Except for one brief note. It was in Naphtali, one of the more obscure of Jacob's sons that ultimately a small village of no particular economic value, military importance or political notoriety was founded. The name of that village, in modern times an extant city of a substantial population, is Nazareth.

Our account is now lacking the inclusion of two tribes, one being that of Benjamin. It was a small tribe named for the youngest of Jacob's twelve sons, and the younger full brother of Joseph. The tribe of Benjamin was given a small allotment, as befit its population, to the southeast of the tribe of Ephraim. For many reasons Benjamin was a tribe that to employ an old boxing term "punched above its weight," producing fine soldiers and many famous men, each of whom was named Saul. The first was King Saul, the first king of a united kingdom, and the second being Saul of Tarsus, now known to us as Christ's apostle Paul.

The story of land division among the tribes concludes with Judah, the largest and as history and Divine will would demonstrate, the most important of the tribes. Judah himself was only the fourth oldest of Jacob's sons, but through the history of the years of this family he had become its de facto leader, and certainly its spokesman. To Judah's descendants a necessarily large allotment was required, and thus the tribe received the lion's share of the southern half of the Promised Land. Not only its population, but its geographical area was the greatest of any tribe. As the years and generations rolled on, Judah, often closely associated with Benjamin, would assume the most prominent and influential role of any of the tribes. Its loyalty to God, although flagging and almost totally collapsing many times, never fully evaporated. It was through Judah that God's original promise of a blessing to Abraham and his seed would be fulfilled.

The initial, military and political phase of the conquest of the Promised Land, now known as Israel, had been fulfilled. For the moment the land and its people had peace, but extended tranquility for the Israel of the Old Testament would never be attained within the chronicle of its pages. God, though, had fulfilled this phase of His promise yet the real eternal promise was as yet unfulfilled. It would come through the tribe of Judah.

CHAPTER THIRTEEN

LEADERSHIP

In reality, even for antiquity, the distance between the land of Goshen, on the eastern edge of the colossus that was Egypt, to this new land of Israel in the east was no more than a few hundred miles at most. Between these two loci, though, was the separation of decades, even generations of time and a historical panoply of events to rival and surpass those of any other nation in history. Between Goshen and Israel, even geographically so much had occurred from the parting of the Red Sea and the destruction of the elite of Pharaoh's pursuing army to the decades in the wilderness and the triumphant campaigns of Israel's army in Canaan. The Law, plain, understandable yet comprehensive and intricate, had been issued by God on Sinai, and neither Israel nor the world could or would ever be the same again. So many changes, earth jolting cataclysmic developments had occurred, and the beaten, bedraggled slaves who lived at the whims of the Egyptians had been fashioned into the fully accountable nation of Israel.

All this was a long time coming, and it happened neither by celestial whimsy, nor by "luck" or by man's hands. Instead the metamorphosis of national character happened under the leadership of but two men, Moses and Joshua. From the Burning Bush on Mount Sinai from which God had called Moses, then a mere shepherd, to the death of Joshua at age 110 the fortunes of Israel were inextricably bound to the personal characters and records of but these two men who had served both Israel and God as the undisputed leaders of the nation. Our test will reveal a large portion of its thesis now, and that is the assertion that such was the character, faithfulness, steadfastness and pure character of these two men that in their absence God would have been compelled to fashion a different kind of salvation for His people, the Jews. Morally and character wise the two men were quite similar, yet personality wise and the particular skill set of abilities which each man possessed was markedly different. Before we proceed with a more detailed examination of the history of Israel itself, we shall now consider the often differing, but often complementary skill sets of these two men.

"Leadership" is a word that is overused, and we write with some trepidation at adding to the glut of the conversation. The shelves, whether real or digital, of modern sellers of books are ever groaning with increasing numbers of volumes devoted to directions and musing on that ever-elusive subject of leadership, be it business, family, political or otherwise. Many are well meant, some are of value, but the majority represents little more than canned platitudes and diatribes. Our belief is that the scriptures, in this instance, a particular section of the Old Testament, is the opposite of such. Neither Moses nor Joshua needs another book, another essay, another sermon, or whatever, extolling their talents and virtues as leaders. Their lives, and the nation of Israel pay adequate tribute to each man. Research and reiteration, though, are needed to show that each man, Godly as he was, was also uniquely well suited for his awesome responsibilities and working with the designs of God each performed brilliantly.

The initial fact of the leadership character of Moses and Joshua is the stark, dramatic distinction between it and the "leadership" of four centuries of Egyptian slave masters. Their leadership was dictatorial, brutal and the leadership of the lash. A Hebrew slave existed to produce for his Egyptian masters, and his failure to so do begin to quickly extinguish his value to the Egyptian leadership. Now even though for the better parts of decades, the Israelites were unappreciative and even rebellious they received leadership of moral integrity, consistency and personal sacrifice. The harsh reality, though, is that they possessed no appreciation and continually resented the slightest difficulty as a problem of gargantuan proportions.

For all the strained comparisons that may be made the relationship of master and slave is not really that of leader and led. Back there in Egypt it was all new for both the Israelites and Moses, but it was not new for God. The Egyptian masters cared little about how they were perceived by the Israelites just as long as their expected tally of bricks was met. Failure met severity, perhaps even death. Moses could not and would not operate in that manner. He and his fellow Israelites would learn together, but unfortunately for Moses (and for the Israelites) he was a better student than they. The task of leadership, with its enormity and responsibility, was new to Moses, and as new as it was it remained unwanted. Although it is often overlooked, apparently Moses never really "enjoyed" being the leader, enjoyment always being a requisite conceit of the modern psyche. He was, though, a man to whom deity to God and to his fellow Israelites was the pinnacle of importance. Israel, not once, never, suffered by any neglect from Moses.

Almost everything which has been said of Moses to this point likewise may be stated of Joshua. Of course, they were two individual men of differing backgrounds and of a somewhat different heritage, but in character, in the nitty-gritty of life and leadership they were of remarkable similarity. An obvious difference, though, is in their presentation and acceptance by the Israelite people. To the core each was an Israelite, Moses from the tribe of Levi and Joshua, a descendant of Ephraim. Their initial familiarity with the nation each would lead was, though, markedly dissimilar. Moses had been away from Israel for forty years, enjoying the tranquility of life as a successful shepherd when suddenly he was introduced to the Israelites as their deliverer from slavery and degradation. Joshua, much younger, had grown up with his fellow Israelites, had himself been a slave and likely in some ways understood the peculiarities and idiosyncrasies of his own countrymen better than his notable predecessor, Moses. From youth he had taken a dynamic, faithful and successful role as a leader of his people, and at least in retrospect appears to have been perfectly placed as the successor to Moses. From an earlier date and a younger age Joshua likely knew the Israelite better than did Moses. No scriptural evidence is found, though, that indicates that Joshua ever became infused with cynicism about the people he was leading. Such would have been and so yet remains anathema to a leader.

Our narrative has already made allusion to the reality of both Moses and Joshua at the early stages of leadership being completely new to their roles, at least outside their own family circles. Newness and inexperience are usually the great parents to mistakes, especially in the field of leadership. Fortunately, though, by the time that both Moses and Joshua assumed their mantels of leadership each was already a mature man, with each being blessed with exceptional ability, strength and moral character. Their "beginner's" mistakes were decidedly few, and each man was ready for his ordained role from the beginning. Moses was plagued by early self-doubts as to his own worthiness and reliability, but how could he legitimately expected to be otherwise? He was not among those few who were accustomed to dealing with emperors, kings and pharaohs. His fears, real though they may have been, seemed to have been proven to be more grounded in inexperience and natural humility than they were in any self-doubt.

Joshua, whether expectant of the responsibility and honor or not, truly was ready to step in as the successor to the great Moses. Unlike Moses, though, his resumé as a leader among the Israelites had already commenced. As one of two spies of hope and optimism, the other being Caleb, Joshua was confident in God's willingness and ability to hand Israel a victory. Unfortunately, he was forty years ahead of his countrymen, but later his same robust faithful obedience to God brought down the famous walls of Jericho. He was a leader who was always in the fore, but perhaps the sheen of fame has never shone as brightly from Joshua as from Moses. Nonetheless along with King David to this day thousands of years hence Joshua remains as one of the two most celebrated leaders in Israel's long national history.

Characteristics of Great Leadership

They were two distinctly different men from different, even radically so, backgrounds, but their leadership traits and methodologies were strikingly similar. At the centrality, the core, the very beating heart of their leadership skills Moses and Joshua shared a characteristic so rare that it can hardly ever be called "common" in any context. Each man had that duality of ability, so rare that it inevitably captures the attention of a studious observer, the twin abilities to both receive and to give orders. The disciple is reminded of a scene some twelve hundred years hereafter where one even greater, immensely so, than either Moses or Joshua, who was confronted by an "authoritative" man desperate for his help. A Roman centurion was tormented by the apparent impending death of a dear servant. The officer, a Gentile soldier immersed in a rearing and life of Roman paganism knew little of Judaism, but he had seen enough to know that a young rabbi named Jesus of Nazareth possessed miraculous healing powers unknown to any mere mortal before or since. He got word to Jesus that his confidence in Jesus's ability to heal was so great that he knew that Christ's word alone was enough to heal his servant. The centurion explained that he himself was "a man under authority" who both gave and received orders. This was a man who Christ praised with effusion and recognized in him a man who could handle both sides of authority. Twelve centuries before both Moses and Joshua proved themselves as prime examples of such men, men who had both the confidence to issue directives and the humility to follow them.

Moses and Joshua each was granted great authority by God, but try as one might the scriptures will not reveal a single instance where that authority was abused or misused. The moral character of each man was so deep and well-formed that authority and power rested easily on the shoulders of each leader. Moses, the most famous figure of the Old Testament, naturally invites and to the eager student commands the attention. Not only was he totally heedless of any notion of aggregating power to himself he was ever eager and ready to utilize his influence for the good of others. We have already recounted his intercession, a ceaseless intercession, for his fellow Israelites, but it invites a closer review. God had become so justifiably angry with

His chosen people that finally He decided to scrap His original plans and grant the ultimate blessing to the personal lineage of Moses, rather than through the recalcitrant Israelites, as originally, He had purposed. Immediately Moses, whose name, fame and grandeur thereby would have radiated even more luminously, stepped in between God and the Israelites and dissuaded the Father from such an action. He had wisely and selflessly "interceded" on behalf of a nation that often had desired to kill him.

So many of history's most famous leaders have made their names and reputations through war. On one extreme is found the renown conquerors of history, men of the stance of Alexander the Great, Julius Caesar, and Napoleon Bonaparte, men whose DNA seemed to be deeply stamped with the need to conquer, subdue and quite bluntly, to kill. The trio cited are among the most famous and successful, but others of their ilk, less successful, are counted in numbers which are legion. They made their reputations and notoriety through bloodshed, copious oceans of blood and war. Moses viewed himself not as a general, nor any sort of inspirational military leader but rather as a conduit and an agent of power, the power of his God. Mose certainly Moses possessed a temper, but almost always he possessed it rather than his temper controlling him. He was a peaceful man, and nothing in the Torah indicates that he was not at his happiest and most content when he was living the quiet, inobtrusive life of a shepherd. Moses was a great leader for many reasons, not the least of which was that he was a man not only in almost total control of his emotions but also because those emotions were proper and valuable.

The great successor to Moses, his protégé Joshua, is not quite as easy to explain and categorize. Like all he had his own heritage, background, personality and experiences. One of the blessings enjoyed by Joshua and one from which he profited immensely was the long-term tutelage of Moses. Moses was sui generis, a man suddenly plucked from forty years of obscurity to become the first leader of his country, a nation still shackled by the charms of slavery. As a subordinate Joshua was a superstar, not only rising to what the moment demanded but even surpassing such a standard. When almost all of his compatriots (Caleb excepted) wallowed in self-pity and fear Joshua beautifully and brilliantly combined a trio of positive qualities, faith, optimism and a general practical knowledge of the situation. His life character, and intelligence had molded Joshua into a man with promise of being an exquisite leader.

Such a leader he was, but unlike Moses, Joshua is not easily described as a man or a leader of peace. He was the man chosen to lead an army of Israelite troops who through experience, tenacity and courage developed into a well-trained and dangerously deadly military weapon. In fact Joshua, along with King David from a future generation would prove to be and yet remains as Israel's two greatest military commanders. The sanguinary nature of the battles which Joshua was forced to fight, the ghoulish bloodletting and "fight to the last man" style have already been discussed. Joshua was the man of Israel most capable of handling this repulsive task, not because of any lust for blood but rather for his assured faithfulness in carrying through even the most unpleasant tasks.

Like any two persons Moses and Joshua had their similarities and their personal distinctiveness. Leaders they were but in heart they viewed themselves as servants of God. With ample time and training, actually it was Joshua seemingly who was more prepared to step into a leadership role. Further he offered no objections to God about his selection, whereas the excuses of Moses were boundless and seemingly inexhaustible. First to

God and now to us over three millennia later they appear as great leaders of their people. But how did they appear to the people whom they led?

Expectations and Disappointments

Leadership, good, true sincere leadership has always been a rare commodity in this life, and likely so it shall remain. The people who are being led, though, have a vested interest and certain expectations of the leaders that they have either chosen or been forced to follow. Ostensibly, the follower, the true, faithful sincere follower has an inherent right to expect certain qualities from the man or woman who is being followed. The list of such qualities is not short, and it differs from person to person. Oftentimes, in some moments, even most of the time, the people do not know what they want, and the basic arbitrary and capricious nature of human beings rushed to the fore. Human desire for leadership is bizarrely inconsistent. Every four years the citizenry of the United States selects a new president as their leader. The chosen man represents one of two parties and generally one of two basic political philosophies. The man chosen on a certain Tuesday in November may be widely extolled, personally popular, radiating with charisma and the darling of the people. Four years later, and sometimes with no appreciable change in character or policies he may have become a tainted object of ridicule, with dismal "approval" ratings and the contempt of most of the people. In those four years he may have not really changed appreciably, but what most often occurs is that the personality and character traits of the people are being revealed for what they always were. So it is in all countries and in all eras.

The obvious and pertinent question to us is crystallized into thoughts of what did the Israelites seek in a leader, especially at the beginning of our story. They were a people who actually had no real or legitimate experience with leadership. Being in that lowest echelon of society, especially in the ancient world, they were oppressed slaves. For some four centuries the Israelites had no leadership. Only harsh slave masters ruled their lives. Their back breaking labor in the searing heat of the desert built the great monuments and treasure cities of the Egyptian pharaohs. In return they were provided lodging, at least a minimal diet and a strictness of rule that would be seen as cruelty to any animal. Management-labor relations were condensed to a quintessence of simplicity – obey or suffer the consequences. That was the "leadership" that had for generations been forced upon Israel. Toil and obey, and you will be kept alive to toil and obey another day. Then one day, unexpectedly to all, Moses arrived after forty years estrangement from his own people and heralded the dawn of a new era, not just for Israel but for mankind and for eternity. Follow your God, he declared, not follow me, and you will receive freedom, a beautiful land of promise and the right and pleasure of living your own lives. How thrilling and exciting such was to the Israelite nation. They had a new leader, the promised removal of their claims and nothing but good to savor in a glorious future. Moses was new, and this mature fatherly figure was the excitement of the day. Such bliss was not sustained, though, between the leader and the led.

The message of Moses was exciting and burgeoning with promise, but Moses as man and as leader was lacking in thrills and "charisma." This is a quality of mankind which has not slackened and eased by the passage of the centuries into the modern age. Without transgressing too far down the roads of time it must be remarked that modernism with loud, incessant media, promotional campaigns and advertising has exacerbated these qualities in the modern person. Just as the Israelites desired excitement in a leader they instead received a mature middle-aged man who would serve as God's spokesman for what God desired of them. Whatever personal "popularity" Moses possessed with his people it did not survive the noonday heat of very many days. Unfortunately, this was not a momentary shock to the nation's system but a way of life and thinking that stretched for many decades. The Israelites of Moses's day remain in history's front rank of people whose expectations for a leader were not really leadership but pampering, coddling and a continual acquiescence to their petulantly childish and often impossible demands. Moses failed not as a leader, but we must be conscious of the principle that those being led likewise have responsibilities. God was freeing the Israelites from bondage, but their natural instincts had drifted and often plunged into a sick detritus of rebellion, hedonism, paganism and always, always childishness. Moses remains not only a Biblical and historical standard for a leader. Unfortunately the people he tried to lead succeeded in becoming a byword for the grossest form of rebellion. Ultimately, though, as so often occurs, his reputation grew as the years elapsed. By the time of the New Testament among most Jews, Moses had become more than a shepherd, a leader, and a spokesman for God. Amazingly, even that short and simple name of "Moses" was used to represent a time, an era, a faith, and a legal and moral system. His name itself was held in awe, and other than Christ Himself, no one's name is more frequently cited in the gospels than that of Moses. For once the people, the populace, had it correct. No mortal man has ever been more deserving of praise, adulation and emulation than Moses.

To employ an old trite remark his successor Joshua was the same but different. Personally and as a leader the faith of Joshua is secondary to no man, including that of Moses. Joshua remains famous and honored, but not as famous and honored as Moses. Much younger than Moses, yet Joshua lived through many of the same times and stresses as did his illustrious predecessor. Still, though, until assuming leadership himself, he lived them in an important, yet secondary position. As with Moses, it is difficult to find events in his life worthy of criticism, and we shall not even try. Whatever the problem, the impediment and the apparent and often the presumed strength of the enemy, Joshua was impelled by a core belief that if God had ordained something to be done, it was, in fact, capable of being done. Literally, Joshua as Israel's chosen leader and its chosen commander, knew that his life was at extraordinary risk and his life subject to being extinguished by battle at any instant. He was not foolish, but neither was be paralyzed by personal fears and doubts. Joshua led and set an extraordinary example of faith, courage and a willingness to sacrifice his life for the Lord's greater purposes. No armchair leader, no behind-the-lines leader and general was Joshua. He was the real thing.

No leader can really remake the people which are his to lead, and Joshua engaged in no such futility. The great leader, though, recognizes who is in his entourage and deals with them accordingly. Here it must never be overlooked that Joshua was in a far better and more fortuitous position than Moses. At the heart of our narrative in the story of the difficulties, ultimately proving insurmountable, which were Moses's burden every moment of every day for forty years. He led ex-slaves, childlike, even infantile, that were proving impossible to produce adult accomplishments. Joshua led no people of perfection, no automatons of obedience, but he led a people hardened by years of living in the wilderness yet never knowing the stain and dehumanization of slavery. In battle he led brave, determined men, and overall, though, Israel was never a model of perfect contentment he led mature men. In short, Joshua was given an "easier" task than Moses, although that word aptly merits the quotation marks it has been given. At the end, when advising his fellow Israelites, admonishing and encouraging them Joshua provided his own epitaph with one of the Bible's most famous statements:

> "If it seem evil unto you to serve the Lord, choose you this day whom you will serve; whether the gods that which your fathers served that were on the other side of the flood, or the gods of the Amorites in whose land you dwell: but as for me and my house we will serve the Lord."

It was not long before this underrated and truly great man died, and Joshua's remains were buried in Shechem.

Joshua was his own man, but wisely he had walked in the steps of Moses, the man scripturally proclaimed as the greatest of all leaders. Now, both were gone, but Israel remained, but it was hardly secure in its Promised Land. Where would it go and what would be its fate?

CHAPTER FOURTEEN

QUO VADIS

A strange paradox exists with many stories when it is realized that so often it is easier to state when a story ends than when it begins. The Holy Bible itself, though, is bereft of such a difficulty inasmuch as its first phase is "In the beginning God created..." and ends with "Even so, come quickly Lord Jesus." Its story has a precise beginning, and its glorious ending is that for the faithful it never ends. Here, though, we have limited our study to the specificity of the Israelites beginning and development as a nation of God's Chosen. Now, though, perhaps a bit tardily for this, the thirteenth chapter, we examine the commencement point of the great story. Our nomination was first announced several thousand years ago when the first chapter of Exodus proclaims:

> "Now there arose up a new king who knew not Joseph."

The story of Joseph and his eleven brothers is so well known and oft told that another rendition is not here necessary. In summary Joseph arrived in Egypt as a teenage slave and through the exercise of his own innate abilities and faith in God, with the enthusiastic support of the Pharaoh, raised him to a position akin to a prime ministership, second only to the throne itself. His brothers came, seeking to fend off starvation, and through the machinations of God, were soon blessed with the status of a welcome, perhaps even favored, family in Egypt.

Exodus, though, in that one quoted verse draws the line of historical demarcation. With a new pharaoh, the Israelites were no longer honored guests but a potential labor commodity. Pharaoh feared their numbers and their potential military might and while he was still able, he turned the Israelites into slaves rather than see them become soldiers bent upon insurrection. Such a tranquility of a scene as a presumed "moderate" slavery was lacking in antiquity, and certainly in the yoke imposed upon the Israelites. The Egyptians had the Israelites build monuments and treasure cities to the Pharaohs on the great Nile, but still:

> "... the more they afflicted them, the more they multiplied and grew.
> And they were grieved because of the children of Israel.
> And the Egyptians made the children of Israel to serve with rigor.
> And they made their lives better with hard bondage, in mortar and in brick, and in all manner of service in the field: all their service, wherein they made them serve, was with rigor."

Hard labor. Long, hard hours. Hard punishment. Endless, unpromising hard lives.

A particularly modern conceit, especially in highly developed prosperous Western nations, is that life itself can be lived at a thrill-a-minute pace, one delight following another, with each day brighter than before. While we should not begrudge prosperity and pleasure, a maturely rational person knows better. At the opposite end of the spectrum is a life with little or no joy and delight. Every day is a shade of gray, perhaps too often morphing into blackness, and life itself provides little pleasure and not much future promise. This, and more, was the slavery in which the Israelites lived their days, days doubtless truncated in number by the harsh physical conditions of slavery.

Not only was their slavery hard, but doubtless it was monotonously boring, a phobia which we moderns possess in massively persistent quantities. One day was the same as the one before and the one after and the one... It was endless, and any alteration of the routine would not be initiated by the Israelite slave but only by his Egyptian master. The monotony, daily, monthly, yearly, by decade, even by century, dulled and repressed the minds and spirits of an Israelite people who were by nature and heritage quite intelligent. Worst of all, the Israelite slave exacted no profit or pleasure from his/her work. It was done solely for the benefit of the Egyptian masters. It was energy draining, mind numbing and soul killing.

The minds and spirits of the slaves were numbed, repressed and deliberately almost extinguished by the tyranny and despotism of their masters. As bad as it was, it was worsened to a far greater degree by the realistic awareness that the lives of their children and grandchildren had not a scintilla of hope or chance of change and betterment. Almost all of what has been related, and much more, is true of societies containing large foundational blocks of slavery in their construction. The slavery of the average Israelite, though, must have been particularly onerous and galling to bear since he knew that he was a descendant of the great patriarch Abraham and that now he labored for the glory of pagan deities and their acolytes.

All the ordinary means of improving and enhancing the lives of one's descendants, the children, the grandchildren ad infinitum were foreclosed to the Israelite slaves. No matter how hard he worked the benefits and fruits of his backbreaking labors accrued not to himself or his family, but to his masters and ultimately a pharaoh, a man who cared not a whit for the lives, aspirations and miseries of his Hebrew slaves. Almost all to the Egyptian masters, all to the glories of the "divine" pharaohs, those most powerful beings in the world, and merely a subsistence penny to the bedraggled Israelites slave. And the slaves knew all this and even more, down to the tips of their gnarled fingers and the emptiness of their hearts. The legacy of the Israelite man and woman to their children was just more of the same. To the average Israelite, with much substance and reason could be exclaimed "I have no hope." For some four hundred years this was the life of almost all Israelites. Thankfully, human chattel slavery has (almost) entirely been relegated to the history books, but not without its first having left massively deep scars on the psyche and character of its human sufferers. The multiplicity of generations of slavery had naturally warped the Israelite character, the character of a special chosen people with enormous reservoirs of intellect, energy and innovation. They had become living, suffering, obedient robots in the Egyptian service of the pharaoh. Hope now belonged to other people and other nations. The part was a memory, the present a memory and the future a dark promise of even bleaker times.

Undoubtedly always there could be found Israelites who desperately wished to change the tragedy of their lives, but the odds against them were so overwhelming that they plunged deeper into depression. Only from outside this unhappy nation could salvation be found, for they could do nothing themselves. The reader is now spared another retelling of the story that this work has already attempted to relate, Moses's appointment as deliverer of the Israelites. Like all Old Testament stories, though, with study and contemplation it becomes to be seen as a foreshadowing of an ever-greater event(s) to come. It is in this light that we hope to catch a glimpse of what enslavement really did to an Israelite man or woman. This is seen by viewing the exodus from Israel of almost one million slaves, historically true that it was, in the more important focus of the eye on its metaphorical, even allegorical, role of all humanity in the spiritual role of an enslaved Israelite, miserable, an infamously "short, nasty and brutish" life and destined for degradation, ignominy and ultimate destruction and oblivion. The Israelite's earthly master was the Egyptian pharaoh, at that point the most powerful man in the world. All humanity, every man or woman born before or after Moses, is subject to the fantastically strong pull and reach of another master. This is the mastery and slavery of the world, sin, and as much as the modern skeptic scoffs, its origin, Satan himself, a sterner and more diabolical taskmaster than any of the pharaohs.

A few, most definitely a very few of the Israelites, realized that their peril deepened and was more potent with each step they took without God. In the beginning, at the height of the frenzy and excitement over the Egyptian exodus they were delirious with freedom. In reality, though, in the words of a Deliverer far greater than either Moses or Joshua and was to appear over a millennium later who lamented that their ancestor's were still as "... lost sheep without a shepherd." Language such as that would certainly be meaningful to the shepherd of a lifetime such as Moses, and the shepherd-sheep metaphor is more than prominent throughout the scriptures. It is the very essence of the relationship between God and man. Without a caring, nurturing shepherd, one who is willing to die for his flock, any sheep or lamb is a piteously helpless creature. Moses was such a shepherd for Israel, yet the people spurned him. God's own Son later became both the shepherd and the sacrificial lamb for all humanity. Christ remains the hope, the salvation, the Good Shepherd, and in the language of our present context the Deliverer of one and all. There is no other. No man or woman born has ever been of a character, a spotlessness or a moral strength sufficient to generate even the first spark on the path to salvation. As the Israelites needed their deliverer Moses all who even draw breath receive salvation by the grace of God alone, solely in the person of His Son, Jesus Christ.

For the moment we refocus our lens upon the Israelites snatched from the bonds of slavery, not by Moses, but by God Himself. In the beginning of what we now call the Exodus exactly what did God expect from them? Among His other attributes God is a realist. Certainly He had no notion of His Chosen people winning their freedom by a great clash of arms, with Israelite forces besting the mighty and experienced Egyptians upon some blood drenched battlefield. This would have been preposterous. The Israelites had zero military experience, were lacking in martial knowledge and skills and would have been little more than targets for the hardened professional Egyptians. God expected from the Israelites what He still expects from the Christian disciple in the twenty-first century and beyond. This is an obedient following in His path and in this particular instance the steps of His anointed leader, Moses. They could do little more, just as the Christians can perhaps do even less following in the steps and Light of Christ. Even this, though, from the very outset, the Israelites declared themselves incapable of doing. When release from Egyptian chains was not immediate and their entry into the paradise of the Promised Land seemingly delayed and perhaps even foreclosed, the muttering, the murmuring and the incipient spirit of rebellion which so characterized them began to assert their vile, poisonous qualities. Those Israelites were a foreshadowing of a section of Christ's later famous parable of the sower. With them the good news of freedom could not withstand the "weeds" which began to grow and suffocate the truth. Early in the story doubtless God knew that He was dealing with the proverbial "stacked deck," and it was the Almighty Himself against which it was stacked. Nonetheless, because He is God, the Creator, He persevered, and the exodus was effected with Moses leading the nation across the dry bed of the miraculously parted Red Sea out of the easy reach of the armies of Pharaoh.

A standard cliché, and like the majority of clichés possessed of much truth, is that children are impatient. So it be true, but far less often is heard the reverse of this pithy expression in the phrase that a truly mature person is patient. After the exodus the basic childish nature of the Israelite people came rushing to the fore. When Moses, by their standards, delayed coming down from Mount Sinai where he was receiving the Law, impatience began to take reign among the Israelites. As he was absent the Israelites began to circulate among the people, the more prominent of which whipped up the anxieties and fears of the multitude and plotted a return to Egypt and slavery. All thoughts, even to an insignificant modicum of submission to God were now abandoned and, in their fore, they would slink back to Egypt with a freshly minted golden calf to placate the pagan proclivities of the Egyptians, now once more to be their masters and slave drivers. Of course the rebellion was quashed with the return of Moses, and some three thousand rebels lost their lives. It was a sadly marked illustration, more vividly expressed much later in the New Testament when the apostle Peter pointed to the proverb's truth of the apostle as one who is:

> "The dog is turned to his own vomit again; and the sow that was washed to her wallowing in the mire."

The imagery employed by Peter should be sufficient to describe the Israelites of rebellion. They were headstrong, petulant, impatient but above and below it all, they were childish, a quality to which they added so many other disreputable traits. So it is in the Christian age (or any other time, for that matter) where so many can never take even the first halting strides towards any sort of maturity. As to the Israelites they left Egypt with the worst traits of children, already described, and time, events and their own stunted moral character only intensified their immoral characters.

It is truly how long the perfidy of the Israelite character lasted through time and troubles, but as yet no triumphs. Children are subject to emotional stirrings of an immediacy which mature adults should have surpassed. Quickly, rebellions and outright insurrections against Moses (really, God) led by rabble rousers such as Korah and Dathan. Even in his own family, with his older sister Miriam, Moses stared into the face of disgruntlement and discontent, but Moses, a magnificently great man, showed love and wisdom by interceding with God to soften her punishment.

One of the prime illustrations of God's frustrations with the Israelites is the snapping of His long-suffering patience early in their exodus period from Egypt. In modern parlance God had "had it" with the Israelites and decided to re-route His lineage of salvation from the line of Abraham, Isaac and Jacob (a/k/a Israel) to the descendants of Moses himself. Too often God had already dealt with the malignant rebellion of the Israelites and in Divine exasperation was now determined to redirect the lineage of salvation through the bloodline of Moses. The latter man, though, modest and meek, dissuaded God from such an action by interceding on behalf of his fellow Israelites. The original line of descent would remain, and it was intended, but the enormous maturity and self-sacrifice of Moses was its Savior. As for Moses and for God the Israelites continued in the childishness of newly emancipated slaves.

As wonderful as may be the glorious and wonderful days of childhood, the playing, the discovery, the learning, the lighter hearts, it is only a temporary abode never intended to be a permanent playground. Still, it is hard to leave childhood, and many persons of all times and climes never do and never even make the effort. This was post-exodus Israel for the better part of two generations and provided the instigation and impetus for many of Moses' greatest dilemmas. Eventually, no matter how self-centered, immature and just plain selfish, most persons are capable of demonstrating growth and maturity. The generations of Moses's time never did, and their self-absorbed whining and egotistic national and personal myopia was never altered until the years passed, and their generations diminished and died. What an epitaph and a legacy for a people blessed with enormous inherent ability, a moral and civil law authored by the Hand of God Himself, that they had to expire and vanish from the living until real progress could be made. Like an unfortunate number of persons of any time and any nation these generations of Israelites grew older but never grew up. A fellow countryman, a self-described Jew's Jew as a "Hebrew of the Hebrews," the apostle Paul perhaps most eloquently gave the description of his fellow Jews as a "stiff necked people." Yet, Paul himself was only quoting from the exasperated denunciations of God Himself who said this at the time of the golden calf.

Few persons in life present a sadder spectacle, a great disappointment, than an adult man or woman who simply does not or will not mature or in other vernacular "refuses to grow up." For two generations these were the people which Moses led, with frustration, anger, impatience and actually more than a scintilla of love. But these generations proved that they could not have subdued the Canaanites and taken the Promised Land. Decades of desert wandering was their assigned lot, hundreds of thousands of lives needlessly wasted and a promised reward denied them. The metaphorical similarities between these early Israelites and the spiritually immature of any generation are obvious, and it is not necessary to belabor the moral lessons. So many of every situation, from the outright evil to the "harmless" decent people never assume any spiritual responsibility in their own lives. Far worse, many, seemingly in increasing numbers deny directly or tacitly that they have such a duty as spiritual responsibility.

Except from afar Moses never viewed the Promised Land nor did he witness his people's entrance into it, but such was not the fate of Joshua. As did his predecessor Moses the career of Joshua cannot and should not be extricated from his relationship of both fellowship and leadership of the Israelite people. But... it was a different Israelite population that Joshua led. An oft referenced truism is that all people are really the same, regardless of race, time and circumstances. This simple expression contains a spine of truth and wisdom, but it does not hold as absolute, undeniable truth. As did Moses, Joshua led the Israelites, a nation of common ancestry, common ethnicity, religion and history, but the Israelites with whom Joshua was charged with leading were different, at times radically so, than those who were Moses's charge. Over forty years had elapsed from the time that Moses assumed leadership to the transition to Joshua. Though their similarities were marked so also were the distinctions, all this according to God's plans. The adult population of Israel which traveled behind and alongside Joshua had already far different influences on their lives than did the generation of Moses, a generation born into slavery, the effects of which they never eradicated. The older of these Israelites had seen and experienced the awe-inspiring miracles of decades ago, the exodus itself and the parting of the Red Sea. While their consciences and psyches were yet youthful these events pressed deeply into their memories, and as a poet since remarked the thoughts of youth are long, long thoughts. This generation had only youthful experience with the taint and degradation of slavery, and they found it much easier to adjust to the ways of free men and women.

An enormous segment of being a free man (and, here, with apologies, is the masculine rather than the feminine since we will be commenting much on military activity) is the assumption of responsibility. The generation which Joshua led into battle and as colonizers in the Promised Land, were required to act with enormous physical and moral courage or die. These were Joshua's "mighty men of valor," and with time and intense experience they developed a military potency to march or exceed any they faced in battle. It would be tediously repetitive to recount their battles and brave deeds, but the Bible and history shows that these Israelites were up to the task. No more than any other was the generation of triumph, but Joshua, with David, Israel's greatest military leader, had the necessary men in number, skills and character which he needed. For the task and the duty they were given, we might borrow an expression from twentieth century America and assert that they were Israel's "greatest generation."

Joshua, like all history's truly great leaders, was a man of and for his times. His succession to the pinnacle of his country's leadership is no surprise historically, Biblically and doubtless it was no shock to his fellow Israelites. His was the onerous and unpleasant duty of leading a nation in war, and in this historical instance truly a "just" war. Almost all wars are denominated just by their originators. Few actually are, but Joshua's call was to lead the Israelites through the mayhem and blood of righteous battle. Military skill, especially in its upper reaches, is a rarity among men. True religion and spirituality is an ever rarer and most precious commodity. Joshua combined the two in a fashion of faithful brilliance such as few men have ever done. He earned the right to be justifiably proud of his famous self-bestowed epitaph that "... as for me and my house we shall serve God."

Separately and together Moses and Joshua were the two extraordinary, faithful and great men that God employed to midwife, give birth and then early nurture to the nation of Israel. Yet, we are compelled to make inquiry "was it worth the effort and sacrifice?" Our next and concluding chapters hopefully will serve, at a minimum, as a pad from which this discussion may be launched.

CHAPTER FIFTEEN

CONQUER AND DIVIDE

After the passage of half a millenium the descendants of Jacob (Israel) had finally returned and were settled into the Promised Land of Canaan. In a myopic political sense this was the triumph of our portending title of <u>The Exodus, Wandering and Triumph</u>, but was this really the triumph of the nation of Israel, the chosen people of God Himself? Whatever the goal and however its definition the "triumph" of the Israelite people was glaringly and dangerously incomplete, and their situation fairly begs for analysis and commentary.

The Israelites who began to settle into this small region in the far southwestern section of Asia were hardly the downtrodden, childish, and lackluster slaves who had made the historic exit from Egypt. Generations of difficulties and hardships had bred into and fashioned a people of strength, even toughness, and they had shown that under good, even historically great, leadership, they were worthy of the confidence and responsibilities that God had placed upon them. The Israelites, perhaps with the total population of maybe one million, were a significant nation and on the battlefield had proven themselves to be a powerful force. Still, hardly could it be touted that Israel was by any means a world power. To its west remained the great dynasty of the Egyptians, perhaps not at the pinnacle of its power, but still a power to be respected and an on-again, off-again enemy or friend of Israel. More immediately this tiny elongation of land in Canaan known as Israel was surrounded by enemies who wished not only to defeat this strange conglomeration of monotheistic worshippers of an even strange God but who really wished to eradicate and exterminate these upstart Jews in their midst.

The nations which surrounded God's Chosen were ubiquitous, numerous and deadly. Especially in its early days Israel's most formidable foe and noteworthy enemy was the nation of Philistia, a land of uncertain boundaries (as were most ancient states) but possessing a long and ferocious warlike spirit. For the most part the Philistines were settled to the immediate west and southwest of Israel in that troublesome area known by the modern name of Gaza.

Central to that hard core of problems faced by Israel in its infancy and early generations is the hard fact that while the Israelites had arrived in Canaan, had won many battles under Joshua, they essentially remained an occupying force, deeply resented by all other nations, and not yet completely victorious even in its own new homeland. Undoubtedly, the Gentiles among whom the Israelites lived and were surrounded, quickly ascertained that these were not the ordinary, run of the mill foreigners. In a vast multiplicity of ways they were different from everyone, <u>everyone</u>, else. They lived by the rule of a codified law, intricately and precisely detailed, a law that was more than the command of a king but one which was based upon moral principles and rights for men and even women, the latter a novel concept in ancient times. To employ a political and historical term which has suffered from a certain modern moral taint. Israel was in many matters a confederacy. A small nation composed of twelve tribes, each with its own leader and locale, at this juncture in its history Israel was operating with a fair degree of unity. Its unifying factors were a common history, a common ethnicity, a common Law of Moses and ultimately the one God. In very real and personal ways Israel too had been blessed with Divinely ordained leadership in men of the highest quality for decades. They were, of course, Moses and Joshua, likely the two greatest successive leaders that any nation in history has enjoyed.

All the above reasons played substantial parts in differentiating the Israelites from its close neighbors and generally all rival nations, but by far the true delineation is that the Israelites worshipped the one true God, while other nations were the homes of convinced, in some cases enthusiastic, polytheists. This was and ever remained the core distinction between the Israelites and their polytheistic, pagan enemies. Ultimately, the Israelites' strength and their very hopes for survival rested upon unity. Their fledgling nation, a relatively small island, in a sea of enemies, was no juggernaut on its own, but unity with themselves and under their leaders was a force-multiplier. Division meant destruction. The real unity, though, that was of incalculable value was a unity of the spirit under the God who had slowly hammered away the shackles of slavery. With no all powerful pharaoh and no man of the prestige or caliber of Moses and Joshua where would the Israelites turn?

The Time of the Judges (circa 1367-1044 B.C.)

Israel had become a nation of some cohesiveness and kept within its proper boundaries was deserving of a realization of pride for its accomplishments in settling into Canaan, albeit even from the onset it appeared to be perhaps just one major slip, one calamitous battle, away from destruction and extinction. As the people began to settle into their new land, their new homes and a new spirit of independence whether or not they had such a realization they had come to their tiny corner of the world at a time of expansive monarchies and empires. To the west still a formidable power was Egypt, a land whose fortunes ebbed and flowed during the long period of antiquity. As was noted earlier Egypt was now rarely a direct threat to Israel, bit its sheer size, prosperity and power entitled it to a continuous consideration, if not necessarily fear in the policy considerations of this fledgling nation of Israel. Egypt proved to be a magnet for wars and for alliances and even protection, from which Israel would often avail itself. In general, but with an exception or two, in these times Egypt was at peace so also was Israel. This was not so with so many others.

The Israelite people lived precariously surrounded by an endless array of hostile nations, each one of which would provide the enemy in endless wars. The most noted and historically renown of Israel's antagonists included the Ammonites, the Canaanites, the Midianites, the Moabites, and most illustrious of all, the Philistines. All were different people, with somewhat different civilizations, histories and abilities, yet they bore much in common. These were all Semitic peoples, all heathen and paganistic to the core and all bore a burning, almost insanely intense hostility to the Israelites, these strange monotheistic interlopers in their midst. (We leave it to the individual reader to draw comparisons to the present state of the modern Middle East). Too, their lands and properties were thickly covered with pagan monuments and idols, tributes to endlessly growing lists of deities that themselves were often merciless, bloodthirsty and even ravenously demanding of human sacrifice. The difference between Jew and Gentile were indelibly impressed upon the times and the historical record. What is more to the immediate point, the Jews were greatly outnumbered in the midst of ferocious hostility. Their great captain and leader Joshua was dead, so what were they to do? In point of fact, though, the real question is what would Israel's God do.

The twelve tribes of Israel, each essentially self-governing, still required the cohesiveness of a central authority. God and Israel thus began the lengthy period of the Judges, extensively covered in the Old Testament and the source of so many of the Jews' great stories and triumphs. The very title "judge" is a slight misnomer. The fourteen men and one woman who became the judges of Israel certainly possessed judicial authority, even as the concept is understood in the modern sense. So much more accrued to their office, though. It was also an executive position, and the people looked to the judges for "executive" decisions of state, even, and perhaps especially in times of war.

Of the fourteen persons who became judges perhaps only six garnered what could be called lasting and historical fame. These were Deborah, Gideon, Jephthah, Samson, Eli and Samuel. Spiritually and morally even these were a mixed lot, although with certainty Deborah and Samuel will always count among Israel's greatest leaders. Those which are unnamed, including the first judge, a man named Othniel are basically draped in Biblical obscurity, at times close to anonymity. A few, though, invite a closer look for their historical prominence and the abilities which they demonstrated while serving the Israelites ad God.

Remarkably in a land that is putatively synonymous with patriarchy the first truly noteworthy judge of Israel was a woman named Deborah, a gentle soul whose "court," such as it was, had its location under a palm tree between Ramah and Bethel in Mount Ephraim where "... the children of Israel came up to her for judgment." Obviously, a highly respected lady, who was also a poet, was shoved into a scalding cauldron of combat when the Canaanites, a well-armed military power, arose and sought the destruction of the Israelites, an apparently likely event. Deborah was not Joshua, but rather a wise, gentle leader, but she had the proverbial friends in high places, specifically Barak, a leader with military capability and experience. Under Deborah and Barak the outnumbered Israelites employed both the elements of weather and the Canaanites' technological superiority against them and plucked an outstanding victory from the gaping jaws of almost certain defeat.

In common with all its moments of celebration that followed, the victory over the Canaanites was short lived. In fact, the Canaanites themselves were far from totally subdued, but the Israelites were so faced with other would-be destroyers. The enemies of Israel were a many headed hydra, each possessed of the will, the striking power, and the venom to destroy Israel. There soon loomed the Midianites, an ancient nomadic people of no fixed dwelling place. Named for Midian, the younger half-brother of Esau, himself the twin brother of Jacob, from the time of the enslavement of Joseph they were a tearing thorn in the flesh of the Israelites. As was so tragically common, though, the conduct of the Israelites itself veritably begged for trouble, as Judges record:

> "And the children of Israel did evil in the sight of the Lord: and the Lord delivered them into the hands of Midian seven years."

The Israelites rebelled, and the Midianites responded with a bloodthirsty vindictiveness and a scorched earth policy which drove many Israelites into hiding, even into caves. By their

EXODUS, WANDERING AND TRIUMPH | 219

own gauge of reckoning the Israelites knew that they needed a "mighty warrior" to rule and lead them, and this time God was in agreement. His choice was Gideon, so "mighty" that God's messenger angel found him secretly in the humble, even ignominious act of threshing wheat in secret.

As the Israelite leader Gideon's first task was to eradicate the earth of his own father's idolatrous statues to the pagan god and goddess, Baal and Asherah. Itself this act was portentous of a difficulty seen in Gideon himself, who for a leader of Israel could have a peculiar blind spot towards idols. Gideon was one of the judges, perhaps even the primary example, upon whom a heavy weight of military responsibility fell, and it is for this, especially for one incident, by which he is remembered.

The Midianites with an army of tens of thousands were joined by their allies, Israel's ancient enemy, the Amalekites, and possessed both the desire and the wherewithal to militarily crush Gideon and the Israelites. Still more the Midianite army possessed the high ground in opposition to the Israelites. Gideon had managed to gather to the cause a total of 32,000 soldiers, a number still significantly lower than the enemy's. Only to God, the Father of Israel and the Creator of the universe, would be the realization that Gideon's problem was too many Israelites. Thus, He ordered Gideon to take all his army down to the Jordan River to effectively separate the wheat from the chaff. Gideon obeyed and listened as God gave him the strange guidance (some might even term it "weird") that:

> "Every one that lappeth of the water with his tongue as a dog lappeth, him shalt thou set by himself, likewise every one that boweth down upon his knees to drink.

And the number of them that lapped, putting their hand to their mouth, were three hundred men..."

Before the United States Marines famously proclaimed that the "Marines are looking for a few good men," God had initiated and perfected the idea. The decisive battle was fought at night and by employing a tactical montage that included noise, surprise and an almost supernatural fear, Gideon routed the Midianite horde, which "ran and fled." The lessons are so numerous still today, but to God's disciples two stand forth in illumination. Obedience, always at the very heart, the pith and marrow of God's commands is once again demonstrated as essential. Secondly, numbers alone never determine the victor, a forceful fact later most clearly demonstrated by the Savior who selected twelve non-descript men as his apostles and who "... turned the world upside down."

As a judge Gideon proved to be a man of inconstancy His life and administration too often showed an acquaintance, perhaps even a flirtation, with idolatry. Yet, in general he was a figure of faith, a strong judge and in that evergreen Old Testament phrase "a mighty man of valor."

With but one exception the next six judges of Israel are men of obscurity, a lengthy run broken only by the notoriety of a judge named Jephthah, not the most famous of Biblical personalities but certainly among the more notorious. He was the illegitimate son of Gilead and a prostitute, and in his early years gained infamy as a sort of freebooter, a leader of a band of malcontents and to put it plainly, "criminals." Most importantly to the moment, though, he was good at what he did and was a soldier and a leader par excellence. He became, as well, the right man at the right time I the right place.

War had erupted between Israel and yet another ancient enemy, the Amorites, and Israel was desperate for a leader, another battlefield savior. Jephthah was approached by Israelite leaders, but he demurred because of his unseemly treatment from the Israelite established leaders, especially those of Gilead. The Israelite leaders, with their proverbial hats in hand approached Jephthah, perhaps the only and surely the most experienced warrior-leader in sight and implored him for his help. Jephthah, still bitter from the past treatment from the Israelites and secured a promise from them that he would be their leader should he defeat the Ammonites. Backed into a corner Israel's leaders assented, and ultimately Jephthah led the Israelites to a smashing victory over the soldiers of Amnon. In the euphoric aftermath of victory, Jephthah, giddy with victory, wildly vowed to kill the first living being to appear from his house when he returned home. Return he did, and was first greeted by his daughter, who would be the sacrifice. A great combat leader was Jephthah, but a foolish, violently whimsical and foolish man.

After the demise of Jephthah the office of judge was filled by a triad of successors, men of no particular import, whose names are found only in Old Testament obscurity, Ibzan, Elon and Abdon. Fittingly, this trio of dim historical lights was followed by perhaps the most famous judge of all. He was not the most important, certainly not the greatest moral exemplary or even leader, and until the last moments of his life a profound disappointment. He was Samson, of the tribe of Dan, and a man of strength and power so formidable that even on the twenty-first century his name is a synonym for masculine strength and power. Blinded by the Philistines he finally achieved earthly immortality by his strength and obedience bringing down the temple of the Philistine god Dagon and killing massive numbers of Philistines and at least one Israelite, Samson himself.

Samson was followed by Eli, a basically well meaning but deeply flawed man who was compromised by his own sins. Eli, though, was a man entrusted by God and a boy's mother in the mentorship of a young boy who would become Israel's last but greatest judge. This was Samuel, raised in the temple itself, and from childhood instructed and inculcated with the history and knowledge of the Israelite people and of their God. From boyhood Samuel developed a deep and thorough knowledge of the Law, the customs, strengths, quirks, and outright sinfulness of his own people. He understood them, loved them but could be disappointed with and perplexed by them. Samuel took his office seriously and records his steadfast devotion to his position by constant traveling to literally issue judgments in disputed cases. Samuel was a true, diligent and hard working as any man who has ever served God in an official capacity. He had the respect of the Israelite people, but a sense of love and affection seemed to be lacking. Also he had the misfortune of being a judge at the very end of a centuries long reign of judges, generally "inglorious" men and women who did not stir the popular sentiment. To the Israelite populace it was eventually time to consign not only Samuel but also the office he held to history's garbage heap. The Israelites wanted what everyone else had, which meant they wanted a king. Samuel was old, he had not the dash of youth nor did he possess the charismatic luster of military victory. The Israelites were aware that their great enemy, the Philistines, was still pressing heavily upon them. Finally, the grumbling and murmuring crescendoed to the breaking point when Samuel's sons, appointed as judges, proved to be corrupt. The leaders of Israel demanded of Samuel:

"Behold, thou art old, and thy sons walk not in thy ways: now make us a king to judge us like all other nations."

Herein is the plaintive cry and the self-pitying cry of the child to the parent expressed as "... everybody else has one so why can't I?"

As would any conscientious normal human being, Samuel was angry and deeply hurt by this spear of ingratitude which had been stabbed into his heart. He, of course turned to God in prayer, and the Lord of Hosts responded with His derisive Divine understanding:

"And the Lord said unto Samuel,
Hearken unto the voice of the people in all that they say unto thee: for they have not rejected thee, but they have rejected Me, that I should not reign over them."

Many centuries later the Son of God would express this same truth when He remarked to His apostles that "... the world hated Me before it dated you."

After Samuel declared to the Israelites that they were about to receive that for which they pleaded, he turned to his last great task as a judge, the selection of Israel's new king. The Israelites were about to start an era of over half a millennium where they would imbibe to the lasty bitter dreg the meaning of the old adage, "be careful what you wish for. You may receive it."

Kings Go Forth

(For a more extensive examination of this important period in Israel's history the reader is referred to the author's 2021 work on this subject, <u>Saul, David, and Solomon: The Perils of Power.</u>)

Israel demanded that it be allowed, even sanctified, with the right to have a lord, a monarch, a single man, a king, rule over them like almost all other nations. This weak and vile symbol of humanity's inability to properly mature is with us yet, but in ancient times it was ubiquitous, with Israel's being a notable exception. To Samuel, old, faithful, wise Samuel, the greatest of all Israel's judges God assigned the task of finding and anointing the new king. Simply on a personal level we may concede that Samuel would have had some resentment at having to effectively midwife his successor. Yet Samuel is not great without substance, for he dutifully obeyed God and headed to the hill country of Ephraim to locate Israel's first monarch.

In Ephraim at this moment was a strikingly remarkable young man who, of all things, was looking for some donkeys that had strayed from his control. Samuel had already received God's instruction to access this man's acquaintance and anoint him the first king of Israel. His name was Saul, and at first, he showed no desire for a king's power and pomp and was content with his life with family and friends, where he was both accepted and admired. From Samuel's own writing we know that if any man ever looked like a king it was Saul. Strong and young, perhaps no more than thirty when first confronted by Samuel, Saul was very tall, Biblically described as a "head" taller than almost all his contemporaries, strikingly handsome, unprepossessing and a model of what many, even in post- and hyper-modern times, view as an ideal man Samuel anointed Saul's head with a vial of oil and promised him that God's spirit would remain with him so long as he served the Lord.

Samuel summoned a large number of Israelites to Mizpah, a city north of Jerusalem, where he expressed his own disdain for them and his disappointment in their desire for a monarch. Nonetheless God would select for them their first king, and his will would be expressed in the casting of lots. Saul, of course, was the name upon whom the winning throw fell. At first, he was nowhere to be found, but soon he was located hiding among the pack animals. Saul, though, was soon extricated from the company of his bovine companions and quickly achieved widespread popularity among the Israelites as a warrior/king who led his men to victories against Israel's many enemies. Soon, even the contempt which the leaders of the larger, more status driven tribes such as Judah and Ephraim, began to jettison their animosity and contempt for Saul, the mere farmer from the small southern tribe of Benjamin. Saul was now both a popular king, and a king with whom the Spirit of God dwelled. Yet, not for long.

Early in his reign Saul began his fall, a long, terrible, destructive tumble in which this not unadmirable man destroyed himself by his self will and later his insane jealousy for his successor, David. David, while not the greatest spiritual leader of Israel, was its singularly most interesting and arresting figure in its history. His life's story is so well known and so lengthy that the current narrative resists its retelling. He, of course, appeared early as a young shepherd who slew the Philistine giant Goliath, saving Saul's kingship, and grew in fame and adulation among the Israelite people, especially the women, by his remarkable combination of talents and character that have rarely been equaled. By his spirit, desires, ambitions and abilities Israel as a nation began to rise in stature and assume its place in the sun. Unfortunately, though, David's reign began a centralization of power, political power that in his aftermath could and would be used by a succession of the worst kinds of kings to destroy most of Israel. David's virtues exceeded his faults, the latter most notoriously infamous by the adultery with Bathsheba and murder of her, her husband Uriah. Of truly great, though, unfortunately not of lasting consequence, is that during David's long reign pagan idolatry never got a foothold in Israel. The darkness of its shadow always threatened this small land, though, and in the reign of David's son paganism would uncoil itself for an extended and destructive stay.

Under the reign of the son of David and Bathsheba, Solomon, Israel would rise to its pinnacle of political status and would made a name for itself in this part of the world. Solomon, employed tens of thousands of workers (Israelites who were little more than slaves) to fashion magnificent structures throughout the small nation, including the splendid and beautifully artistic Temple in Jerusalem. It was the most elaborate and exquisitely beautiful of Solomon's projects, and the Israelite people were justifiably proud that their presumed center of worship was the equal, if not the superior, to any such structure in the world. Such a magnificent building, its construction denied to Israel's most famous and greatest King David, required a formal dedication, and David's son was certainly equal to the task. Seven years of labor, countless backbreaking labor were required to construct this edifice, which was covered in gold and breathtaking in its splendorous beauty.

Solomon set a day for its dedication, the beginning of a time of worship and the offering of literally tens of thousands of animal sacrifice to God. The king himself offered a dedicatory prayer to God and then a speech to the great assembled multitude in which God, Israel and perhaps a bit of Solomon were lauded, literally to the high heavens. Israel was at the apogee of its ancient Biblical glory. The days of slavery and the Egyptian exodus and the wilderness wanderings were receding and fading from the national historic memory. Israel had arrived and had its place in the sun. Certainly it was not Egypt, nor could it be reasonably compared to the later great empires such as Alexander's Greco-Macedonian and the Rome of the Caesars. This geographically pinched nation with its strange people, strange laws and even stranger God, had become a legitimate regional power, a potency with which other countries had to contend. Most definitely Israel was at the zenith of its power, many conquests in its recent past. To utilize the Biblical metaphor Israel appeared as a bright glowing light in a world of darkness. The high noon of Israel would now begin its fade, sometimes slowly but sometimes with startling swiftness, into a division of national obliteration and to some Israelites a return to subjugation.

The reasons for Israel's fall do not necessarily provide a specific date, time or person, but they invite an opinion or two from the interested observer. The temple was finished and dedicated in the mid 950's B.C., and so in many respects was Israel. Solomon was the king, an enormously powerful man, and he should bear neither the blame nor the opprobrium for others sins. His alone were great enough. His overriding fault was so great that in some respects it still overshadows his other great sins, although none are really disconnected one from another. Born into royalty and comfort, he had an insatiable appetite for wealth, luxuries and the lifestyle that came from it all. His appetite for women was even greater, and Solomon remains are history's greatest abusers of the Fourth Commandment. He collected upwards of one thousand girls and women as wives and concubines, and his sensual appetites seemed resistant to boundary.

Still, it is for one overriding fault, a great sin against Israel and God, that Solomon is remembered. He opened the doors of Israel to pagan idolatry, an idolatry that destroyed the bulk of the nation and had its virulent effects with the remainder. This began the ignoble "conquest" of Israel. It remained true, though, that Solomon's reign was a time of prosperity, pomp, even glamor, and Israel had the iridescence to the world of a bright, sparkling jewel. So have other nations at other times, and the historical among us are reminded of the words of the last king of France whose life and reign were untouched by the cataclysm of the French Revolution which erupted in 1789. King Louis XV, enjoying the pomp, power and luxury of the absolute monarch of Europe's most powerful nation once famously remarked, "Après moi, le deluge," or in English "After me, the deluge." Following Solomon's death the reigns of total destruction began.

CHAPTER SIXTEEN

COLLAPSE

Under wise King Solomon the nation of Israel reached its zenith of earthly glory. The land had been modernized and beautified by new structures built at the monarch's direction and by tens of thousands of Israelites who labored for the great monarch's glory in conditions akin to abject slavery. Israel was a respected nation in its part of the world, its trade and commerce vastly increased under Solomon, a nation to be accorded respect, at times perhaps even fear. Israel was at its mountain top, and cliché ridden as it may be, its only trajectory was descent. Its downfall came in many stages, at times dramatically, often slowly and inexorably, but it never recovered its geopolitical standing it "enjoyed" under Solomon.

Solomon lived luxuriously and with all the accolades and wealth which antiquity provided its ancient rulers. But like all men and women his days in this world were rapidly and inexorably expiring. His apparent and preferred successor was his son Rehoboam, but this prince was not accorded universal acclaim among the people. Rehoboam had a brother with the rhymically lyrical and similar name of Jeroboam, who desperately wanted the throne. The story of these two brothers' conflict is well and thoroughly told in scripture, but for the purpose of our narrative let us race to its denouement. Simply spoken, but with underlying complications, the ten northern tribes favored Jeroboam, and only the two Southern tribes, Benjamin and the largest Judah wished Rehoboam to be king. Thus the nation which Moses had led from Egypt had severed itself into two, Israel and Judah, two countries with a common heritage, a common ethnicity and at one time a common law, but now going their separate ways. Their first two kings likewise were harbingers of the future fates of the two monarchies. Rehoboam, the actual legitimate king, was hardly an endearing figure, arrogant, with a heart already hardened towards his own people, but he had the aura and the stamp of legitimacy. Jeroboam was a skillful opportunist who began to plunge the northern kingdom of Israel into a pagan cesspool from which it never escaped. It is perhaps not coincidental (if there really is such an event as a coincidence) that Rehoboam's and Jeroboam's reigns and personal and monarchial characteristics of what was to come for their respective lands of Judah and Israel, the latter being the one to which we first turn our gaze.

Expressed harshly and starkly but with sad truth Israel, the northern kingdom, never had a decent king. This fact was exacerbated by the reality that the northern tribes of which Israel was composed were almost always weaker and more prone to idolatry than was Judah. That is a strong denunciation of Israel, but as history would show it is also a very weak compliment to Judah. So many bad kings, so many lapses into the temples of idolatry that the ancient northern kingdom has historically become a byword for apostasy and the lapse into idolatry. A study of the Old Testament reveals this small, truncated version of Israel seemingly competing with its own history to attain new lows. For notoriety its nadir was most declaimed when Ahab, an

Israelite, became king and delivered into history a byword for evil in the person of his wife, the Canaanite interloper and then queen of Israel, Jezebel. Their confrontations with the great prophet Elijah provide one of the Bible's most pulsatingly interesting periods. Nonetheless, this was but a moment in history as Israel, with its political, military and spiritual fluctuations, its ups and downs, eventually succumbed to its own internal weaknesses, spiritual apathy and rebellion, and collapsed as an independent kingdom and nation.

A small nation, always riven with strife and plagued by rebellion, poor leadership, and endless battles against its neighbors, Israel as an ancient nation effectively breathed its last in 722 B.C. with the burgeoning, cruel and hyper-aggressive power of the north, Assyria, overrun the country and cruelly, even viciously, reduced the Israelites to slavery and took them away to reside in its own Assyrian Empire. Throughout history and a type of historical mythology these ten tribes have often been denominated as the "Lost Tribes of Israel." While such a designation radiates a certain mystic aura it is really untrue. Most of the Israelites were simply absorbed into local Gentile populations by intermarriage. Actually, the Assyrians did not take all the Israelites, and many were left behind, specially in the middle and northern ranges of the country. They, too, usually intermarried with local Gentile populations and became known as the Samaritans, a people of great Biblical, especially New Testament prominence. All these Israelites were the conquered, and they themselves made no conquests. The history of the northern kingdom of Israel was marked in 722 B.C. as "finished."

Judah

In so many ways Judah was a preposterously small nation, a political entity which was no more than the alliance of the two southernmost of the twelve tribes, the largest and most important Judah itself, wherein lay the city of Jerusalem, and Benjamin, a very small tribe which had joined itself to the fortunes of Judah. Together they were the southernmost of the Israelite people who originally wrested control of the Promised Land of Canaan from the panoply of Gentiles who there resided. Of more than minimal importance is the fact that the first three, which is to say the only three kings of a united nation of northern and southern kingdoms, all come from the south, Saul from the tribe of Benjamin and David and Solomon from Judah. Modern political parlance would reference Judah as a "rump" kingdom, in actuality a small enclave of a couple of leftover tribes that either could not or would not remain integrated with the political structure of its northern brothers. Only a few thousand square miles of territory, with its share of deserts and its eastern border itself the very fitting and ominously named Dead Sea. In spite of its disadvantages, its size, and assorted woes, in Judah was legitimacy. It was here that the royal line first established by God with young David resided lay. Upon the death of David and then his son Solomon, when the sands of turmoil and conflict had sifted down to a few tenaciously clinging grains it was David's grandson, Rehoboam, who became king and kept life in the royal lineage. Three millennia hence it would be gratifying to record that Rehoboam was a good king, a fine Godly man whose character and reign strengthened Judah. Alas, though, the opposite is more to the truth.

Rehoboam's reign commenced in the 930's B.C. and an early proclamation from the king himself set the tone of his monarchial stint. Early in his monarchial tenure bluntly he announced to his "subjects" (and this is how he viewed them):

> "(H)e spoke to them after the counsel of the young men, saying,
> My father made your yoke heavy, and I will add to your yoke: my father also chastised you with whips, but I will chastise you with scorpions."

For Rehoboam there were to be no platitudes, no pandering to the people, and certainly no political pusillanimity. He meant to rule as an authoritarian despot, and in this he was successful.

For seventeen years Rehoboam ruled Judah, and driving this span a border war erupted with their Israelite brothers to the north. Rehoboam well proved himself to be a "chip off the old block" a worthy royal successor. Unfortunately, though, his model was not his grandfather David, but rather his father Solomon. During his reign King Rehoboam took to himself eighteen wives and sixty concubines, through which he had sixty daughters and twenty-eight sons. Even more importantly, pagan idolatry through his tiny kingdom did not wane. Rehoboam was succeeded by his son Abijah.

This work and this chapter especially makes no pretense at being a history of either Israel or Judah, and the Old Testament itself, is forever the text from which that truth is drawn. Our interest, though, lies in both summary and in contrast, that being a contract with its northern neighbor and one-time historical cohort, Israel. Judah could be bad, very bad, and the one true God was often displaced by the people's fetishism with idols, yet Judah was never given over totally to idolatry. Most of Judah's kings were bad, several indifferent, but unlike Israel Judah was blessed with at least two great kings, Hezekiah and

Josiah, the latter perhaps the greatest leader politically the people had enjoyed for a span of centuries. Most of the time idolatry had a strong foothold in Judah, and Josiah was the king most serious and successful in his campaigns for its eradication. Actually, along with idolatry, the people of Judah had gradually succumbed to idolatry's close companion, religious ignorance. By the time of Josiah in the early 600's B.C. all transcriptions of the Law of Moses had seemingly vanished, and knowledge of God's will was apparently lost. Then, a portion of the Law of Moses had seemingly vanished, and knowledge of God's apparently lost. Then, a portion of the Law was discovered during a refurbishing on the Temple, prompting King Josiah to launch a nationwide campaign for spiritual revival, which enjoyed much more than a modicum of success.

Even under Josiah, though, Judah was more than a religiously reclusive kingdom. It was a tiny entity buffeted by larger powers, empires even, from all directions. Most particularly the Egyptians to the west and the rising Babylonian Empire to the east had little Judah as a pawn in the never ceasing game of international power. In spite of kings such as Josiah and his ancestral predecessor Hezekiah, great prophets of the stature of Ezekiel and Jeremiah, Judah finally fell to Babylonian aggression under the famous King Nebuchadnezzar in 587 B.C. The Temple was looted, and the majority of Judeans forcibly taken eastward into Babylonian captivity.

Babylon and Nebuchadnezzar seems to be an almost calamitous fit with Judah and its God. Babylon was and yet remains thousands of years after its fall a synonym for opulence, wealth, extravagance and sin supercharged to its full capacity. Little Judah was that strange nation placed enticingly in the midst of great empires, and ultimately it was unable to defend itself from conquest. Monotheistic, explicitly moral, or at least so by design, it was a poor, pitiful fit in the rapidly expanding Babylonian Empire under King Nebuchadnezzar. This man was a brilliant success, a flamboyant tyrant who lived by his own very loosely draped moral code. He was, as were all of his ilk, a polytheist who worshipped multiple deities, not least of which was himself. Yet he was cunning, and his own self-interest coincided with wise decisions. From Judah he selected the finest youth to be trained as administrators in his royal government, and among them were four young men named Shadrach, Meshach, Abednego, and the most influential, Daniel. All four more then met the expectations of the great king, and their stories are firmly emplaced in the superstructure of Old Testament history. The four are especially to be noted as that rarity, men who attained high office while never abandoning God. Nebuchadnezzar remained a fierce, volatile tyrant, a man given to his temper and never a disciple of the one, true God. That same God, though, utilized this King, and while he reigned the Judean people were respected, and their religious practices remained inviolate.

Nebuchadnezzar was succeeded by his descendant Belshazzar, a hedonistic fool who witnessed the famed "handwriting on the wall," but for him and Babylon too late. Babylon's sun had set, and it was succeeded by the empire of the Medes and Persians, one of history's greatest and most influential political entities. The Persians (whom we now call Iranians) built a great civilization and generally ruled with an even, temperate hand. They controlled an empire that numbered 127 provinces and at its zenith spanned from India to Ethiopia, in size and power surpassed in antiquity only by the Roman Empire at its apogee. The Judeans were but a tiny fraction of the populace under Persian sovereignty, but generally they were well treated. Still, they were disliked, if not hated by many and persecuted by some. Persia, though, mighty as it was, would not serve us the final stop for these descendants of those Israelites who so many centuries past were led by Moses in their exodus from Egypt. In 538 B.C., by reason of royal proclamation from the great King Cyrus, these Jews in Persian exile, now only a pitiful remnant of the nation, were given royal leave to return to Judah. Slowly but surely the remnant of centuries of history straggled back to what was once longingly and almost reverently referenced as the Promised Land. Geographically and topographically the land was essentially unchanged; however, so much alteration had made Judah and certainly its one-time neighboring brother of Israel. The great, majestic capital of Jerusalem, the City of David itself, was a shell of its earlier magnificence. The Temple was in ruins, stripped of its wealth and treasures by the Babylonians. Judah was still Judah, but now to its north uncomfortably lay the land of Samaria, the home of the mixed ethnicity of the northern Jews of Israel and various Gentile. The seeds had already been sown for Judah and Samaria to become increasingly bitter enemies, in spite of, or maybe because of, blook kinship and much shared history and culture. The northernmost fringe of the old united kingdom was called Galilee, a region of undefined borders and undefined importance. It was the remaining legacy of the lands of Naphtali and Zebulun, two of Israel's least significant tribes. Galilee was a rough, crude backwater with little history of its own, and certainly little significance or expectations for the future. Further, at the time of Judah's return from Persia it was inhabited mainly by Gentiles.

Still, the remaining descendants of Jacob's sons had returned, but the centuries had changed them and their governmental structure. They resumed their adherence to the Law of Moses to which in its greater parts they had remained true in Babylonian and Persian exile. Much had been jettisoned or sometimes just obliterated throughout the long ordeal of semi-slavery to foreign Gentiles. They were reduced in number and inhabited only a tiny block of non-descript territory in southern Palestine. Any pretense of national glory such as in the days of Kings David and Solomon now rested firmly in the realm of memory rather than aspiration. Judah was, in geopolitical terms, a tiny, rather insignificant nation, and its first and foremost desire had to be mere survival. The world was still ruled by giant kingdoms and empires. Their names may have changed, and the balance of power shifted, but it was still the old, old story of the rule of power and might. Judah possessed little of either.

Back Home Again

The rolling by of the centuries certainly had changed Judah in so many ways, a number of which have been noted. Politically, militarily and its role in regional affairs had been altered, often forcefully, and ultimately beyond recognition. The realm of the spiritual, though, was the arena in which the alteration and change of the national character was most marked. Commencing with those distant days of Egyptian slavery hose chosen of God had too often succumbed to the allure and supposed charms of pagan idolatry. From Egypt, Canaan, Philistia and many points between the people of Judah had abandoned their Creator and, in that startling, but ever apt Biblical phrase, had gone "whoring after false gods." Finally, blessedly, heathenism had dropped from the national conscience, and worship was now to the one true God. By no conceivable standard is that to be interpreted that Judah had become a spiritual jewel, but rather far from it. Paganism and its obscene worship practices, though, had been jettisoned.

Judah, though, still had to confront a world of paganism, and in the 330's and 320's B.C. it received a shock to its body politic when a large professional army from southwestern Europe descended upon the land. They were the Macedonians, led by their fantastically ambitious and shockingly young ruler and general, Alexander of Macedon, forever to be known as Alexander the Great. Judah was summarily gobbled and ingested by these Greco-Macedonians, and it become but another "minor" province in Alexander's great empire which stretched from Europe and North Africa all the way into southwest Asia and as far away as India. If there is a thing as glorious in an empire won by oceans of blood, Alexander's was the most glamorous of antiquity. Alexander himself, though, a whirlwind and dynamo, took sick and died in 323 B.C. at the shockingly young age of thirty-two. It was not a necessarily happy event for the Jews, though, who in his short reign had come to respect the young Macedonian. Almost pathologically ambitious Alexander as a conqueror had been wise enough to keep hands off the practice of the local religion, so long as it interfered not with the affairs of state and empire. Alexander was gone, but his empire remained. In time it was divided into three sections, and initially Judah fell under the rule of the Ptolemies, the dynasty which had ruled Egypt for centuries. Geopolitical matters, though, whether ancient, medieval or modern, are rarely, if ever, static for long. Eventually little Judah was shuffled off to the care and suzerainty of the Seleucids, a Greco-Syrian line which obviously had an extensive power base on this part of the world.

For an extended period of time Judah enjoyed the temperate rule of King Antiochus III (241-187 B.C.), but in time the Seleucid Dynasty, including Judah, fell under the iron rule of Antiochus Epiphanes IV, perhaps the least known vicious tyrant who has plagued the history of humanity. Epiphanes (the title by which he shall be noted) had both delusions of grandeur and the moral compass of a venomous snake. He saw himself as an Alexander, a conqueror and world ruler, and soon was besotted by ambitious dreams of confronting the newly risen great power of the west, Rome in distant Italy. The upstart Epiphanes, though, was humiliated before his own army by an emissary of Rome in 167 B.C., and his heart and intentions were now hardened against all Judah, its religion and its people, whose strange and presumably recalcitrant ways he blamed for his humiliation and setback against Rome. As an absolute ruler he declared the absolute destruction of the Jewish people.

Long before Hitler and the Nazis Epiphanes served as a historical role model for anti-Semitism. With Satanic cruelty and fanaticism he unleased his minions of bloodshed and destruction against the Jews. No descendant of Jacob was immune or exempt. It is difficult at times to glean from the mind of a psychopath and discern his true purposes, but Epiphanes' actions provide us with a certain foundational certainty. This Seleucid Herod saw in the absolute destruction of the Jews the elimination off a problem, an eradication of an entire people whose different beliefs, manners, customs, and most of all their God impeded his path to his empire's unity, a unity whose strength would impel it to greater conquests and perhaps a challenge even to mighty Rome itself.

Epiphanes was well on the road to success. Thousands upon thousands of Jews, including mothers with babies, expectant mothers, children of all ages were slaughtered, often with a barbarity which likely brought a smile to Satam himself. Nothing and no one seemed to stand in the path of Epiphanes and the total, final destruction of the Jewish people. Living yet, though, was an aging Jewish priest who had five sons.

The Maccabean Resistance

The decade of the 160's B.C. had come to this tiny land of Judah and with it an ominous darkness. Epiphanes had marked its people for tribute, extortion and ultimately extinction. A royal Seleucid officer had come to the home of the patriarch Mattathias one day, and for the purpose of bleeding him and his family dry. The old man, though, was cut from an especially powerful cloth, and the Seleucid official was killed. With exquisitely emotional inspiration he rallied his five sons and told them that the extinction of Judah and the jews was in sight, and not on some distant horizon, but now at this moment. If that nation's remnant of the masses which Moses had long before led from Egyptian slavery was to survive, Mattathias declared, it was in the hands of God and his own five sons.

The sons of Mattathias were called to a duty so harsh, extreme and unpromising that it rivaled in difficulty the commission given to Moses by God. Uplift and lead a small, insignificant nation, against the yoke, a yoke of death, being imposed by a megalomaniac leader of an impressively powerful empire. Impossible it would seem, but herein lay the beginning of a dynamic period of ancient Jewish history rivaled by few, if any other, such moments. Under the five brothers, led by the middle sibling, Judas Maccabeus, the sons of Judah rallied and through a series of wars, which cost Judah dearly, their freedom was won. Led by Judas ("the Lion") they defeated their Seleucid oppressors and drove Antiochus Epiphanes IV and his vainglory into exile. It cost the lives of many Jews, including their leader, Judas Maccabeus, but at long last Judah was free.

Judah, that little surviving truncated bloc that was all that remained of the Israel of David and Solomon was not the Israel of old. War, especially the wars as desperately fought as the Maccabean transforms its survivors and the contesting nations, whether win or lose, are often altered beyond recognition. Judah had developed a pride in itself, a still burgeoning swelling of a combination of relief and satisfaction that they were triumphant in a vicious war against a far stronger enemy. For century upon century, the abiding theme of the Jewish people, often expressed in specifics, was that they wanted to be like all other nations (recall their demand for a king). The weights on the scale of national desire, though, began to slide in the opposing direction. Perhaps for the first time they become proud of being Jews, the seed of Abraham, God's Chosen People, and among other matters turned with attentive, at times fanatical, attention to their special status, their Law and the supposed degradation of all other people, the dread Gentiles.

At last the children of Abraham had at least a semblance of political independence, their own land, government their "personalized" God and perhaps so much more, but did they have peace? The Jews turned inward and among other subject employed their more than considerable skills to their religion. Unfortunately, over time they were easily victimized by the spirit that has marked the disciples of God to the present day the spirit of sectarianism. The Judean leadership began to crystallize into several groups, all at odds, but the two most noteworthy being the Pharisees and Sadducees. Not all clashes were purely theological or academic, though, and civil war occasionally flared, most notably in the mid 60's B.C., when the brief, bright period of independence was darkened until its terminus. A power greater than any the ancient world had seen was soaring to its very high pinnacle, and in 63 B.C. the powerful forces of Rome under its political and military superstar, Pompey the Great, entered Jerusalem, tramping into the Temple itself. The independence of the ancient kingdoms of Israel and Judah was extinguished, and never again would be its own sovereign state under its own God. When Rome itself, plagued by endless civil wars, finally morphed from a bedraggled republic to the Roman Empire Israel/Judah, now simply called Judea, became one of its many provinces by early in the first century A.D.

The Judea of the Roman dynasty was neither a placid nor a contented land. For several decades it was a cauldron of internal and external strife, an endless maelstrom of factionalism and threatened, insipient rebellion which finally became reality. Unlike most of Rome's provinces Judea could never come to terms that it was a conquered people. In the 60's A.D. unrest had given way to rebellion, which finally gave place to open and bloody war against Rome and its legendary armies. By 70 A.D. Judea had been brought to bay, and its capitol of Jerusalem, swollen in population by so many Jews seeking shelter from the advancing Roman legionaries. The Roman's final campaign and thrust against Jerusalem has been well and thoroughly chronicled by historical writers and even with specificity by New Testament predictions. In 70 A.D. Roman armies under general, later emperor, Titus broke through the city's defenses and engaged in a butchery and bloodbath, rivaling anything this world has ever seen. The city's walls were crushed, buildings leveled, the Temple itself razed to the ground, and the city streets ran red (literally, not figuratively) with the blood of butchered Jews.

The surviving Jewish people were dispersed throughout many lands to become a wandering ethnicity itself. What Moses had begun and followed through with the exodus from Egypt and crowned by Joshua's triumphs in many battles had reached extinction. Their story of exodus and triumph ultimately was not rewarded and crowned by the conquest of its own Promised Land, however small or non-descript. In a geopolitical and historical sense it is easy for humanity to perceive

God's great plan for the Jews as a titanic slow-motion failure of epically huge disappointing proportion. No lasting conquest of Canaan for certain, but our story remains haunted by the question of whether the conquest of the Promised Land was the real prize. Whatever the level of prize, though, it was quite temporal in nature, having expired for good in 70 A.D. Of course the modern state of Israel was found and recognized in the year 1947, but it is a nation, like all others, with no direct lineage to the Israel of the Bible.

CHAPTER SEVENTEEN

MORE THAN CONQUERORS

They are splayed across the early pages of two of the most famous books ever written, the New Testament gospels of Matthew and Luke. "They" is actually a list or a roster of the names of men, names which in the main are hardly euphonious to modern Western ears. The majority are noted in these two accounts and then promptly disappear into historical and Biblical obscurity. They include such as Joram, Ozias, Joathem, Achaz, Salathiel, Abiud, Azor, Sadoc, Eleazar, Matthan, Melchi, Naum, Nagge, Maath, Semei, Joanna, Rhesa, Neri, Addi, Cosam, Jose, Melea, Mattatha, Saruch, Ragan, Cainan, Sem, Jared and many more named by the gospel writers but equally obscure. Their lists, though, include somewhat more famous personages, such as Adam, Abraham, Isaac, Jacob, Judah, Boaz, David and Solomon. The genealogical chronicles of these two great gospel authors arrive at the same destination, an equally obscure young couple in a non-descript Galilean village in the late first century B.C.. The names of the young man and his even younger bride did not remain equally obscure, though. Joseph and

Mary were the penultimate names in the lengthy genealogies (so vitally important to the Jewish people) which began with creation itself. Only a few of these men possess fully developed literary and Biblical stories, and this brief work has attempted to relate to our these the cogent parts. The story of the great patriarchs Abraham, Isaac, Jacob, and Judah is set before the commencement of our narrative, wile Kings David and Solomon are major Old Testament figures and around whom large portions of this essay are structured.

As for the other men (not a fully inclusive list) they were born, lived and died in Biblical obscurity and except for their brief mention by Matthew and Luke, anonymity. Unbeknownst to them, though, their lives' lasting importance was just as great to God and any of His disciples as were the lives of Biblical and Israelite giants such as Moses and Joshua. No one could rightfully diminish the central, vital roles of men such as Joshua, David, even Solomon, but especially Moses in the history, development, struggles, and brief conquests of His chosen nation of Israel.

The title of this work is at least partially self-revealing and self-explanatory, Exodus, Triumph and Conquest. It is a window into a key portion of a special nation's history, and its first two elements almost account for themselves. Now, in our own time, this continually self-admiring twenty-first century A.D. the Exodus of the Israelite people from Egypt in the second millennium B.C. remains one of history's most transcendent and fascinating events. At least until very modern times the courage and the ability of Moses in exercising God's powers to humble Pharaoh, the most powerful man on earth, and remove the shackles from the Hebrew slaves still stirs all but the most hardened and cynical heart. The miracles, including especially the parting of the Red Sea, will be told and retold so long as our Earth remains a going concern.

Israel and later Judah with all their problems, the negligence, the rebellions, the insurrections and the quite visible vein of juvenile, even childish, behavior running through their history knew triumph, victory, even at times what the world calls glory. After all, with God's favor and the steadfast and brilliant leadership of Joshua the Israelites, the freed descendants of generations of slaves, established their presence in the Promised Land of Canaan. It was never really a complete victory, but in general they had obtained the land promised to them by God. "Conquest" is a term of strength, power, dynamism and above all coming with a strong implication of permanence. Israel's "conquest" of Canaan was not only temporary, but always shaky, jittery and an accurate map would plainly display the porousness of the conquest. Assyria, Babylon, Persia, Macedonia, the Seleucids and finally Rome tramped in and out of Israel, sometimes at their own will and often at the will of God Himself. The seed of Abraham maintained no lasting conquest of Israel, and even if they had what would have been their earthly reward? Constant wariness, surveillance of possible, even probable enemies, and non-stop fear of being engulfed by any of a large number of powerful enemies who had readily identified this area as ripe for conquest.

Israel was a small dagger of territory reduced later to Judah, no more than a tiny square of land which was relatively speaking small change for any one of many voracious empires. Most of the land was arid or at best semi-arid, it was possessed of a remarkably smooth coastline which lacked good ports and harbors was a deterrent to maritime commerce. Its population was talented, intelligent but small, even relatively tiny in numbers, and besides they had little history of cooperation, much less unity. The ancient sojourn of the descendants of Abraham in Canaan was the furthest most remote concept from a "conquest." Still, though, so many, many centuries before God had called out Abraham (then named Abram) from the remote, exotic land of Ur of the Chaldees to begin a remarkable journey that was meant to guide the very trajectory of history itself. Had the Creator of the Universe backtracked, even reneged from the great promises he had made to Abraham? Already, long before the first century A.D. had expired not only Israel's conquests, but Israel itself had disappeared. The original promise and covenant God made with Abraham is so vitally important that it merits a plunge into early Genesis to extract it word-for-word:

> "And I will make of thee a great nation, and I will bless thee, and make thine name great; and thou shalt be a blessing."

The Lord was not slack in His promises to Abraham, and all His promises came, albeit at times slowly, to fruition. As much as any nation Israel had its ups and downs, its divisions, its vicious infighting, throughout its history. All this and more, but it had the solidity of leadership in such as Deborah and Samuel and the temporal glories of kings such as David and Solomon. The land was the scene of a stirring regeneration and rebirth in the second century B.C. under the Maccabees. Exodus, triumph and victories, but conquest? No, for as the historical record discloses Israel eventually collapsed. Even to the staunchest and most faithful of believers a question looms and cannot be hidden. Did God partially fail in His promises to Abraham? To fully study this inquiry and to answer the question the original promise to Abraham must be consulted for its second phrase:

"And I will bless them that bless thee, and curse him that curseth thee: and in thee shall all families of the earth be blessed."

As the years, the generations and the ages wore on it is an inescapable reality that the Jewish people began to have a myopic view of this promise and prophecy. They were, in fact, a special people to God, but not necessarily in the fanatical fashion they came to believe. The blessings were upon Abraham and his descendants, the Semitic peoples of whom the Jews certainly counted themselves. Yet perhaps the key phrase in the blessing is in its final wording that "... all families of the earth shall be blessed." We are called upon to penetrate a mystery, though, a mystery which the Jews of the latter Old Testament and of the New Testament had converted to a certainty, i.e. that the Jews themselves and their nation of Israel (or later Judah) held and in some instances still hold a blessing separate from the entire Gentile worked in which they dwell. Certainly God was true to the Israelites while they obeyed Him and remained faithful, but no people has ever been shunned by God as often as the Jews.

Assuredly, the nation of Israel broke the shackles of slavery and eventually triumphed, although temporarily and intermittently over many nations. Yet it is questionable as to whether these victories, or conquests, provided any lasting glory or benefit to Israel. Our modern eyes and hearts are not immune to the debility that almost always plagued Israel and still has in its fierce hold almost all the world's population. It is that myopia we have noted, a short-sightedness to view everything in material, temporal terms rather than the spiritual and eternal. Most definitely God made a promise to Abraham and to Israel, and He never failed to deliver on those promises. Often overlooked though, is another promise which the Lord made to Israel's great patriarch Abraham. After assuring Abraham that his own descendants would be as numerous as the stars in the sky or the grains of sand on the seashore God gave to Abraham his most important pledges; one worth another reminding quotation:

> "In thy seed shall nations of the earth be blessed; because thou hast obeyed My voice."

"All" nations the skeptical and proud Israelite would have replied questionably? As the generations passed and toppled one upon the other and certainly by the times when the era of B.C. changed to A.D. the Jews had turned inward and were proud, often inordinately and improperly proud of being Jews. It is not unfair to aver that to many, if not most Jews, especially those holding power and influence, the rest of the world was accursed, and in their frequent terminology all Gentiles were "dogs." So how could Israel have achieved any point even remotely resembling a conquest. This tiny slice of land was nothing but a relatively insignificant sliver of territory in the fringe of the great Roman Empire. Its exodus and triumphs were in the dim dark past, the glorious days of Moses, Joshua and David were but hallowed memories. The heel of the Roman boot rested upon Judea. In spite of it all, though, God had promised that through Abraham and his lineage all nations of the earth would be blessed. In God's great Abrahamic promise it is incumbent upon us to focus and define two terms, that being "all" nations and "blessed."

The ending rubble of Israel provides a weak reservoir in which to discover any blessing. The Jews themselves were further scattered to the four winds in their famous Diaspora. By 70 A.D. there remained no sovereign state of Israel, be it slave or free, no Temple and no homeland for its people, all of which are barren resources to comb for any type of blessing. Besides God had promised that "all" nations would be blessed, not just Abraham and his family, the Israelites, the various Semitic peoples, the Asians, Africans, Europeans or those peoples who would come later speaking in "accents yet unborn," a phrase courtesy of Shakespeare. God did promise the land of Canaan to the people of Israel, which they received and eventually squandered. Yet, it would seem strange that an eternal promise from Heaven itself was confined by the borders of a semi-arid land on the eastern shore of the Mediterranean.

Deep into the epistolary portion of the New Testament the apostle Peter stated plainly that "The Lord is not slack concerning His promise." In Abraham's seed all nations, all peoples of the earth were and are blessed, but the Jews themselves are a piteously few in number. The stories we have attempted to recount in this work are to many persons stirring and inspirational indeed, and interest is ever present in the study of these magnificent events and towering persons. Still, the interest is limited to a relative few, and any conquest is of strikingly limited scope and duration. The true conquest did not adhere to the staff of Moses nor to the sword of Joshua (neither of whom was a lineal descendant of Abraham) but rather to that long list of gloriously obscure names of a genealogy related a few pages back. These men and their equally obscure wives lived in what some would call the darkness of obscurity, but to their Creator nothing dark marked their lives. Undoubtedly, most lived what the English poet Thomas Gray called "... the short and simple annals of the poor." No proclamations of thrilling military campaigns, inspirational victories or the luxurious life of palaces marked their existence. Certainly, it would be a grave mistake to say that they in any fashion lived idealized existences. No doubt, this long genealogical list contains a rogue or two, as it would be an almost impossibility that any line of descent was without blemish. They all were totally oblivious to the knowledge that each of their lives, their marriages and their children were links in a Divinely ordered chain that stretched from Creation to Eternity. Except for a leavening of famous names such as the early patriarchs and a later king or two they were totally unprepossessing. Yet, it is through this line was being transmitted "conquest," not the bloody, temporal and often ephemeral conquest of battle but the most important and deadly enemies of all, sin and death.

God's next revelation of triumph and conquest came almost two millennia following His summoning of Abraham from Ur of the Chaldees. The harbinger of the real conquest was the angel Gabriel who appeared to an unknown teenage girl in the downtrodden village of Nazareth in the obscurity of a backwater Roman Province of Galilee. He began to speak to her with a beautiful promise but not that of conquest:

> "Fear not Mary: for thou hast found favor with God.And behold, thou shalt conceive in they womb, and bring forth a son, and shall call His name Jesus.
> He shall be great, and shall be called the Son of the Highest: and the Lord God shall give unto Him the throne of his father David.
> And He shall reign over the house of Jacob forever; and of His Kingdom there shall be no end."

The Christian disciple and even the intelligent fair-minded believer immediately grasps that Gabriel was speaking of the advent of the Savior and the true conqueror, Jesus Christ, for whom Mary and Joseph would be the earthly lineage and who finally delivered God's promised blessing to Abraham. God saw that the battles and struggles in the Old Testament were a necessity, but surely the promise to Abraham and his descendants could not be fulfilled by a relatively few square miles of hot, semi-arid territory in an obscure corner of the ancient world. The conquest had to be more, and its promise was borne unknowingly generation upon seemingly endless generation until Mary delivered the baby in whom all possibility of conquest, deliverance and reward was fulfilled. The descendants of the patriarchs Abraham, Isaac and Jacob were special and especially vital to God's plans. The Jews are as important to God as ever, but likewise are the Gentiles as remarked by Christ's greatest evangelic apostle Paul who stated that "... there is neither Jew nor Greek... for you are all one in Christ." He freed us not from our histories and heritages but from the oppressive artificiality of the constraints which man places upon his fellow man. When Moses and Joshua so capably and faithfully led the Israelites from slavery to victory in many battles the pinnacle of success had not been attained. They were the precursors, the forerunners, the antetype of the true conqueror, whose Divine writ extended past the Egyptians, Canaanites, Philistines or any other temporal earthly society. The Sons of God and He alone faced and defeated the two great enemies of man, sin and death, and as assured by Paul again "... we are more than conquerors through Him that loved us." The sting of death and Satan's "victory" of the grave were smashed with the coming and the mission of the true Deliverer of the Jews and of the Gentiles. Perhaps the first to notice, however dimly and faintly, was Moses on the afternoon when he saw upon Mount Sinai a bush that burned yet which fire was never extinguished.

www.ingramcontent.com/pod-product-compliance
Lightning Source LLC
Chambersburg PA
CBHW062157080426
42734CB00010B/1724